BENOIT

Wrestling with the Horror that Destroyed a Family
and Crippled a Sport

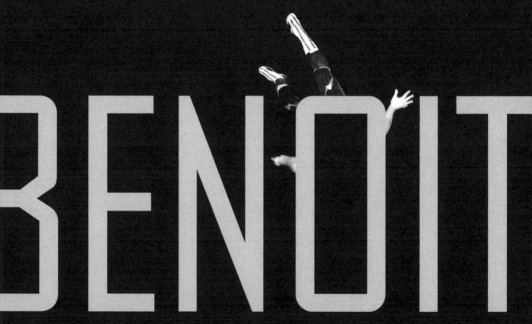

BENOIT

ESSAYS BY STEVEN JOHNSON, HEATH McCOY, IRVIN MUCHNICK AND GREG OLIVER

Published by ECW PRESS
2120 Queen Street East, Suite 200, Toronto, Ontario, Canada M4E 1E2

LIBRARY AND ARCHIVES CANADA CATALOGUING IN PUBLICATION

Johnson, Steven, 1957–
Benoit: wrestling with the horror that destroyed a family and crippled a sport /
Steven Johnson ... [et al.].

ISBN 978-1-55022-812-0
1. Benoit, Chris, 1967–2007. 2. Wrestling. 3. Wrestlers — Canada — Biography.
4. Murder — Georgia — Fayetteville. 5. Suicide — Georgia — Fayetteville.
gv1196.b45b45 2007   796.812092   C2007-904878-1

Editor: Michael Holmes
Cover Design: David Gee
Text Design: Melissa Kaita
Production and Typesetting: Rachel Brooks
Printing: Thomson-Shore

With the publication of *Benoit: Wrestling witht he Horror that Destroyed a Family and Crippled
a Sport* ECW PRESS acknowledges the generous financial support of the Government of Canada
through the Book Publishing Industry Development Program (BPIDP) for our publishing activities.

Canada

DISTRIBUTION

CANADA: Jaguar Book Group, 100 Armstrong Ave., Georgetown, ON L7G 5S4
UNITED STATES: Independent Publishers Group, 814 North Franklin Street, Chicago, IL, U.S.A.
60610

PRINTED AND BOUND IN THE UNITED STATES

ECW PRESS
ecwpress.com

ACKNOWLEDGMENTS

Steven Johnson wishes to thank Rich Tate of GeorgiaWrestlingHistory.com, which hosts archival material related to the Benoit case. On a personal note, his wife Cynthia supports and encourages his work.

Heath McCoy would like to thank the following for sharing their insights on Chris Benoit, before and after the tragedy: Bret, Ross and Keith Hart, Bob Leonard, David Meltzer, "Bad News" Allen, Gama Singh, Milad Elzein, Gerry Morrow, Mike Shaw, Ben Bassarab, Nattie Neidhart, Bill Adomski, Vicki O'Neill, and Kathy Stockland. Another important source was the interview he conducted with Benoit in April 2004. His work is dedicated to his wife Tamara and their beautiful daughter Bronwyn, who was born just before this book went to press.

Greg Oliver would like to especially thank Dave Hillhouse for his contribution from 2 Cold Scorpio, Chris Schramm and Marty Goldstein for making sure Nancy wasn't forgotten in all this, and J Michael Kenyon for the historical aspect of murderers in wrestling. As well, his wife Meredith and son Quinn deserve praise for allowing dad to hide in his cave to get this done.

CONTENTS

ACTIONS SPEAK LOUDER THAN WORDS: THE TARNISHED LEGACY OF CHRIS BENOIT

ACTIONS SPEAK LOUDER THAN WORDS: THE TARNISHED LEGACY OF CHRIS BENOIT

Greg Oliver

Chris Benoit was a man in search of an identity when he arrived in Extreme Championship Wrestling (ECW) in 1994.

He'd had his international successes, particularly in Japan, and had stuck a tentative toe into the North American waters on occasion, but he had never established any sort of a beachhead.

ECW was a wild place, with wrestlers using baseball bats wrapped in barbed wire and tables set alight with lighter fluid. But strangely, the rabid fan base of the Philadelphia-based promotion appreciated the finer arts of professional wrestling as well.

Benoit, with his crisply executed, technically sound maneuvers, fit in perfectly. The passion he had for his craft was obvious. Equally clear was his lack of confidence on the microphone, the missing direction in his career. *Pro Wrestling Illustrated* had even noted Benoit's "dry image" in a 1994 scouting report: "Lack of glitziness hurts him in the eyes of some U.S. promoters."

He would find both confidence and direction thanks to an unfortunate accident.

It was November 5, 1994, the big *November to Remember* show, and he was taking on one of the most wild high fliers on ECW's roster of misfits and castoffs, "The Homicidal, Genocidal, Suicidal" Sabu. Like Benoit, Sabu had a burning desire for pro wrestling. Born Terry Brunk, his uncle was Ed Farhat, better known for the terror he struck as The Sheik, a headliner from the 1950s to the 1970s.

What should have been a routine, though fierce, battle ended in near tragedy when Sabu fell awkwardly, landing on top of his head. He suffered a bruised spine and nerve damage.

Benoit cried in the dressing room, worried for his friend. He left Philadelphia that night, not knowing that Sabu's neck was all but broken. He followed up once he returned to Edmonton, calling ECW boss Paul Heyman, who was over the moon with excitement.

"It's great, you're going to be called The Crippler. This is awesome, we're going to make so much money," Benoit recalled Heyman telling him excitedly. All the while he just wanted to know the status of his friend. Benoit still grappled with the potentially lethal mistake years later. "Things do happen, accidents do happen. I think the people that I work with know me, and the people that know me personally know I'd never take advantage of a situation or someone in the ring like that," he said. "They know that it was a mistake. Things happen. It's a physical, contact sport, and injuries are going to happen." Still, he would admit to liking The Crippler nickname: "It grew on me and I'm proud of it."

The accident led to the persona of The Crippler — and it wasn't really that far off from Benoit's real personality. He was a no-nonsense guy who took his craft seriously. You messed with him, there could be serious repercussions. He wasn't one for distractions either and had an excellent ability to focus. "When I have a goal, I try to have tunnel vision to that goal," he once said.

The ECW run of Chris "The Crippler" Benoit lasted less than a year, ending in mid-1995. After a June World Wrestling Federation (WWF) tryout, where he lost to Sparky Plugg, Owen Hart, and Adam Bomb, Benoit was basically done with ECW, frustrated with the irregular paychecks and the difficulties in getting Heyman to act and complete the working visa he needed as a Canadian to live and work in the United States. Then in August, Eric Bischoff and World Championship Wrestling (WCW) went on a bit of a signing spree, taking Benoit, Dean Malenko, and Eddie Guerrero from ECW to damage the competing, upstart company. Benoit was also bound by loyalty to New Japan Pro Wrestling, which had a working relationship with WCW.

Unlike his brief, previous stint in WCW in 1993, Benoit would be a featured performer for many years. A multi-time champion and a member of the prestigious Four Horsemen faction, he was given the company's world title (just days before departing for the better-known WWF in January 2000). In short, he accomplished a target that he laid out in 1997: "My main goal is to establish myself in North America, and I really haven't had that opportunity because I've been over in Japan for the last eight years."

Gary Juster was in charge of business affairs at WCW at the time, and he signed Benoit to his first contract. Benoit arrived in his office with his oldest son, David. "Chris was always the consummate gentleman, always very respectful, very deferential, always very pleasant to deal with. He was really like that for as long as I knew him," said Juster.

He brought to North America a number of unique wrestling moves that would become synonymous with his career. "I like maneuvers that stun quickly and can be just as quickly capitalized on with, either, another hold or move or a pin," he told *WCW Magazine* in May 1993. "The Snapmare suplex is like that. It hits a man so fast, he doesn't know what happened to him, and he's a sitting duck for the next move — the German suplex. Well, it's athletic instinct to react one way when you're caught in a full-nelson. But to find yourself suplexed to the mat, your body just doesn't expect it, and you're totally helpless at that point. There's no defense."

As a part of the Four Horsemen clique of Ric Flair, Brian Pillman, and Dean Malenko, and later former Chicago Bear Steve "Mongo" McMichael, Benoit had a high-profile role even if title belts eluded him. "People will ask me, 'How does it feel to be a Horseman?' If I think about the tradition and all that, what the Horsemen have been about, it's an honor," he once said. Benoit knew enough to be quiet and listen to the advice of stars such as Flair and the retired Arn Anderson. "Just hanging around these guys hearing them talk was very educational, just being there. I kept my mouth shut and inhaled everything they said and talked about, and learned as much as I could," he told Silvervision.co.uk.

The Horsemen and Kevin Sullivan's Dungeon of Doom faction feuded for months, and Benoit was paired up with Woman (Nancy Sullivan, Kevin's wife) onscreen, which led to an offscreen relationship as well when the Sullivans divorced.

By the spring of 1998, Benoit captured his first wcw title, the tv belt. A best-of-seven match series with Booker T elevated both men. "It was a highlight reel," Booker T recalled to Silvervision.co.uk. "It's got a lot of nostalgia, just two guys *mano e mano.* They were the matches that put me in the limelight as far as being a viable singles competitor. With these matches nobody could doubt me any more." Runs with the tag team titles, alongside Malenko, and stints with the more prestigious United States belt would follow.

While in wcw, Benoit was allowed to keep up some of his international bookings, especially in Japan, where he'd been a big name earlier in the decade. He was considered homegrown talent in Japan, as he had spent more than a year in the New Japan dojo system in 1986–87, improving his craft. The first

PHOTO: MIKE LANO

Benoit as Pegasus Kid in Japan, versus Hiroshi Hase, January 1991.

six months at the dojo were spent doing isometric exercises all day, such as squats and push-ups. After that, the students had the discipline to enter the ring to further their training.

"When he initially got pushed, he got pushed really hard. He was pushed as Pegasus Kid; he won the [International Wrestling Grand Prix] title in 1990 under the mask," explained Japanese wrestling expert Zach Arnold. "Then they re-pushed him as Chris Benoit, as Wild Pegasus. They gave him a couple of IWGP title shots. He didn't win. They pretty much used his character as a mid-card strong character to introduce new guys. They introduced Eddie Guerrero as Black Tiger through him in '93." Benoit said in 1995 that there wasn't any significance to the Pegasus Kid name, that it was just a name that he and "Tokyo" Joe Diago, a New Japan talent scout and trainer, came up with in Calgary.

In his autobiography, Guerrero talks about his first match with Benoit, which happened in Japan. "I liked Chris from the moment we first shook hands. He was totally cool, one of the nicest guys I've ever met. But when the time came to get into the ring with him, I was nervous as shit, even a bit intimidated. I'd seen him work. I knew how good he was."

The pinnacle of Benoit's many successes in Japan were the wins in 1994 and 1995 in the prestigious Super J Cup, highlighting lighter-weight wrestlers. Benoit himself once called the 1994 win the greatest honor he ever had, but wouldn't brag about it in interviews. "It meant a lot to me, as you say, the best junior wrestler in the world," he told Silvervision.co.uk. "I never think of myself of being the best or the quickest. I don't look at it in that way, because to me wrestling is a form of art. It's like when I was in the J Cup, I thought this was great. I never thought this would springboard me to something here, or springboard me to something there. To me, I appreciate the moment I'm doing it in. I don't think beyond that moment, so it was a great accolade for me at the time, but I knew I was coming back again on the tour and had something to prove on the next tour."

Another graduate of the New Japan dojo, 2 Cold Scorpio (Charles Skaggs), ended up teaming with and facing Benoit dozens of times. Competing against someone so many times makes you closer, he said. "Chris and me . . . in this business, everybody has that certain someone that you have chemistry with. To us, we could have had a so-so match, but to everyone else it was great."

Though it was in Japan that Benoit was best known, he would always assert that his time in Mexico made him a better wrestler, opening doors for him to work in Austria and Germany in the early 1990s when the North American promoters wouldn't look at such a small man. "It was a great experience. I enjoyed my time down there. It's a different style of wrestling, a different brand of wrestling, which I think helped better myself in terms of working in the international scene at the time," said Benoit, who was a regular in Mexico from 1991 to 1994, often masked as Pegasus Kid. "I have so many good memories of working down in Mexico, not only from in the ring but outside, and camaraderie with the guys. Some of the guys . . . barely were able to speak English and I couldn't speak Spanish, and having that bond and forging relationships was really neat." In Mexico's Universal Wrestling Association (UWA) promotion, Benoit had a long feud with the Blue Blazer, a masked Owen Hart. He also held the UWA Light Heavyweight title in 1991, upsetting Villano III (Arturo Díaz Mendoza). Benoit and Villano III would feud for months, and their battles climaxed in a historic mask-versus-mask match on November 3, 1991, at the Quatro Caminos Bullring in Naucalpan, which Benoit lost.

In an interview with the Web site SLAM! Wrestling, Benoit explained that he did have a hard time adapting to the ring style in Mexico. "On my first tour I kept trying to wrestle their style, trying to find that medium, and it just didn't work. By the last week I started wrestling my style, but working within their brand of wrestling, and it just clicked. . . . It's faster paced. It's go, go, go, whereas in the States the psychology is different in terms of telling the story."

Chris Jericho (Chris Irvine) was in Mexico with Benoit on many occasions, and he said that Benoit's successes in North America and abroad influenced many, many wrestlers and "changed the style of pro wrestling in this country, because he spent a lot of time in Japan and kind of integrated the Japanese style, the Mexican style, and the hard-hitting Calgary style into the WWE and the WCW, the former company he worked for."

Working in Europe in the early 1990s forced yet another change in Benoit. "The wrestling in Europe is so different," he

Benoit and Chris Jericho.

said. "It's run by rounds, so you have five three-minute rounds, and you'll be in the middle of something and the bell will ring, and you'll have to go back to your corner."

Back in North America, things weren't going smoothly in wcw, which Benoit later said was a "company that was very poorly managed and had very poor leadership if any at all." Behind-the-scenes matchmaker Kevin Nash once dismissed the likes of Benoit, Malenko, and Guerrero as "vanilla midgets," and in 2006, Nash still stood by his comment in an interview with *The Pro Wrestling Torch*. "I love Eddie [Guerrero] and Chris [Benoit] to death, but those guys were mid-card guys thirteen years in the business in wcw. I mean, they're great and probably two of the best workers ever, but they never [main-evented] anywhere else, so I don't know why they put them on pedestals [on *Raw* and *Smackdown!*]."

The constant turmoil behind the scenes of the promotion was having its effect on Benoit and his close colleagues. In January 2000, Benoit finally won a world title, beating Sid Vicious to claim the WCW World Heavyweight Championship at WCW's *Souled Out* pay-per-view. A day later, he surrendered the belt and left the company, headed for the wwf along with fellow "Radicalz" Malenko, Guerrero, and Perry Saturn. "I think everyone was frustrated. Eddie was sick and tired, Dean was sick and tired of it, all of us were," Benoit said of the exodus. Kevin Sullivan had also been elevated to a power position.

The wwf — later known as World Wrestling Entertainment (wwe) — was a wide-open field for Benoit: new opponents, new titles to win, new television shows on new stations, and, finally, the chance to wrestle for hometown crowds in Alberta. "The Rabid Wolverine" reveled in it all, and became one of the company's top performers, reliable in and out of the ring, fighting back for his position regardless of injuries minor or serious, such as a broken neck in 2001.

"No matter what promo we gave him or whether it was written for him to win or to lose, he never complained about anything," recalled former WWE writer Ranjan Chhibber. "Benoit wasn't an avid talker, but he talked to me the most when I asked him about his time in the Land of the Rising Sun. He was proud of his time there and put every Japanese wrestler I inquired about over. And when Benoit praised someone, you knew he meant it, because if he didn't like someone, he would just remain silent about them."

WWE champion John Cena agreed, calling Benoit "iron clad" on *Larry King Live*. "He was real quiet. He kept to himself. He had ultimate respect for his workplace. He was a model employee."

Benoit succeeded in spite of his weak interview skills, fashioning much of his persona after Clint Eastwood in the *Dirty Harry* movies or as "The Man with No Name" in the spaghetti westerns. "He was a guy who maybe wasn't the most articulate human being in the world, but if you watched the facials and the body language, he said so much with that, that he didn't have to say it verbally," said long-time pro and current trainer Les Thatcher.

In January 2004, Benoit entered the *Royal Rumble* as the first competitor, and outlasted all twenty-nine other competitors to earn a world title shot. He chose to challenge for Triple H's WWE World title at *WrestleMania XX* in New York's fabled Madison Square Garden, in a three-way match that pitted him against both Triple H and Shawn Michaels. The whole company was pleased that Benoit was going to win the company's top title, Michaels wrote in his autobiography: "Chris Benoit is a guy who really loves what he does and who wanted the title as badly as I did. Chris is also one of the most genuine human beings I've met in this business. Chris deserved this moment, and Hunter and I were determined to do our best to let him enjoy his reward."

In the end, Benoit made Triple H submit to the Crippler Crossface. Confetti fell from the ceiling, and his best friend Eddie Guerrero, the world champion on the *Smackdown!* program, came out to offer his congratulations in an emotional moment. "It felt like a dream. I was standing there at *Wrestle-Mania* in Madison Square Garden with my best friend in the business, a man who is as close to me as a brother, both of us carrying the gold," Guerrero wrote in his book. "But as soon as the right moment came, I got out of there. It was his night in the spotlight, something that he so rightfully deserved and earned for himself. Chris deserved that title for so long. He had it in wcw for a moment — literally. I know back then I wasn't close to ready to be champ, but Chris most definitely was."

Benoit's family would then enter the ring, his father, Michael, tripping on the way in, his sons, David and Daniel, embracing him, his wife, Nancy, wiping back tears. "The roar of the people went right through us. The people were giving their gratitude to Chris not just for winning the match but for how much all three of those guys [Triple H and Shawn Michaels] had put into it," Nancy Benoit told the *Edmonton Sun*. "Everything was happening in slow motion. His dad was hugging me and his grin was so huge. I've never seen a prouder dad."

"That was a defining moment in my career," Benoit later said, making the rounds of a hungry Canadian media, eager to celebrate one of their own. "I had all these thoughts going through my mind. Visions of training with Stu Hart, my first matches in Calgary and Edmonton, those years working on the road, going to Japan, Mexico, Europe, wcw, ecw, wwe. It all just flashed before me. I'm so happy it happened when it happened, though. A hundred years from now, at *WrestleMania 120*, they'll look back and see Chris Benoit made Triple H tap out at Madison Square Garden. It was such a huge event that carried so much meaning, it's hard to find the accurate words to describe it."

Though Benoit would only hold the world belt until *SummerSlam* in August 2004, losing to Randy Orton, it forever placed him on a higher plane in wrestling history. Not unexpectedly, his career never hit those heights again. He was, however, a professional about the transition. "There's always guys coming into the industry, and I feel I've got things to pass on to them and people who I haven't wrestled yet. Young guys who I aim to help out," Benoit once said. "When Randy Orton won the title at *SummerSlam* I was disappointed that I lost, but I was very happy for him. That's one guy who's going to be a future star in this industry, and I had the honor of wrestling with him."

His last couple years in WWE were full of soul-searching. In November 2005, his best friend Eddie Guerrero died suddenly in a Minneapolis hotel room. His heart gave out after years of steroid and drug abuse. The whole Guerrero clan considered Benoit part of the family, and they grieved together.

Benoit's heart was never the same either. He shared some of the pain in an e-mail with me a few weeks after Guerrero's death:

Hi Greg, thank you for your e-mail. I know that he has left us but I still feel like I'm going to see him on the road next week. I do not know if I will ever have as good a friend as I did in Eddie. I was able to talk to him about anything in my life, and he was always able to make sense of things or change my perspective. Whatever I was going through or whatever issue I had, Eddie would never point his finger at me. He would use situations that he had been through in his own life, times when he had hit rock bottom, and could not immediately change the problem, but how he brought about inner change which helped him accept the situation and better cope. I believe in God and I do pray, but I could not quote any of the scriptures off the top of my head. We would be on 250-mile drives and Eddie would have his Bible open quoting scriptures and talking about different passages. Anyone else and I would jam on the brakes wherever we are and they would be walking. But Eddie had such a way of applying them to whatever we were talking about and make so much sense of everything.

He was somewhat of a spiritual guide for me. I do not know if you read the Bible at all, or what your beliefs are, and I will respect you for whatever your beliefs are. But if you ever get the opportunity to read about Job, it reminds me so much of Eddie. All these tragedies happened to him. He at one point after coming out of rehab had nothing but the clothes on his back. He had physically, mentally emotionally and monetarily hit rock bottom. He lost his family, his wife and children had left. But he never lost his faith and through it was able to overcome the odds.

Instead of Eddie becoming bitter, Eddie became better. In our business it is really difficult to understand why we do what we do and why we think what we think unless you are in it, unless you have a passion for it, it is so demanding physically, mentally and emotionally in every possible way, but when you love it as did Eddie, as I do myself, you have a better understanding of why we do what we do. I do not believe that I will ever find someone that I will bond with and be able to understand and be understood as I was with Eddie. I'm not looking forward to going back on the road, not that I ever did, I hate the road, but I looked forward to Eddie's company and camaraderie. Both of us hated the road, being away from our families, but both of us lived for that in-ring bell-to-bell time.

My wife Nancy bought me a diary and I have started to write letters to Eddie, it may sound crazy but that is how I'm coping. I'm sorry if some of this e-mail does not make any sense either but it helps me cope. Thank you, Greg.

Chris

"I think everyone handles stress differently and Chris was one of those guys that internalized everything. You could see it. Especially after the death of Eddie, you could tell, I could definitely see a difference in Chris and I used to ask him, 'Are you alright, man?'" the WWE's Ken Kennedy told *The Sun* (UK). "Because I used to see him and he had that thousand yard stare, he just looked like he wasn't happy, and I remember I used to call him 'Cyborg' because the pain that that man would endure in a workout, or in the ring, was amazing. It was like no human being could do that."

Life on the road was getting to him too. Colleagues often talked about his love of family, his two children from his first marriage in Edmonton, and his son Daniel with Nancy in

Atlanta, his adopted hometown. "An amazing man," Dawn
Marie told *The Pro Wrestling Torch* in February 2006. "I could
never imagine him doing anything wrong to his family. Loves
his family. Great confidante. If you have any questions, any
problems with anyone, you can go to him." It wasn't uncom-
mon for Benoit to switch his travel plans just to spend time at
home, jetting to Edmonton from Denver before heading to
Atlanta, or flying from Jacksonville to Atlanta for some quality
time before an event the next night in Orlando.

In a July 2006 e-mail to me, having returned to the road
after shoulder surgery, Benoit addressed the stress of the road:
"We were even warned about our conduct when we are out having a few beers. Sometimes we can get a little rowdy, especially
when we are overseas. Apparently someone video-taped a few
of the guys acting up on their cell phone and posted it on the
internet. So much for privacy."

The list of other deceased colleagues kept growing as well:
Black Cat (Victor Marr), who was a trainer in the New Japan
dojo; "Bad News" Allen Coage, who got Benoit booked into
Japan; Biff Wellington (Shayne Bower), who was a championship tag team partner in Calgary; and colleagues, such as Shinya
Hashimoto, Owen Hart, "Bam Bam" Bigelow, and Davey Boy
Smith all died before they were forty. Curt Hennig was forty-
four when he died. Johnny Grunge's death at age forty, in
February 2006, of a complicated mixture of an enlarged heart,
acute toxicity from prescription pills, obesity, and sleep apnea,
cut deep. Grunge (Michael Durham) was also a neighbor in

Atlanta, and their families hung out. For Brian Pillman, Benoit would appear on three of the four Brian Pillman Tribute shows in Cincinnati, stealing the show at the third event with an epic battle against Steven Regal (now known as William Regal). "The hair on the back of my neck still comes up when I watch it," said Thatcher, the event's organizer.

Despite the negative aspects of the business, Benoit kept an eye out for future stars. In 2006, he was strategically placed alongside Gunner Scott (Brent Albright) in a storyline that got derailed when Benoit went off the road to attend to Nancy, following her neck surgery. "I'd really looked up to Chris for a number of years and figured it was an honor to be introduced as his protégé," Scott told PWMania.com. "It was basically going to be the Tommy 'The Machine' Gunn/Rocky storyline, so I'd be working both alongside and eventually in a feud against one of the greatest wrestlers in the business."

Benoit always had his eyes out for talent that wasn't run-of-the-mill. Trevor Murdoch credits Benoit for his employment with wwe. "Chris was one of the guys that helped get me my job. I got a great opportunity to go to Japan for six months, learn the stretches and the bridges. I came in to do a tryout and started doing some of that. Chris recognized it, asked me where I worked at, who trained me. Of course, with Harley Race's name, he went to [Talent Relations boss] Johnny Ace that night and told them to make sure to get a good look at me. From then on, I got my job; every time I'd see Chris, he was asking me how I was doing, if I needed help with anything."

The last, lengthy feud of Benoit's WWE career was with Montel Vontavious Porter (Antonio Banks), over the U.S. title. A relative newcomer to pro wrestling, MVP grew by leaps and bounds working with a master. In a 2007 interview with IGN.com, MVP praised Benoit. "There's nobody more intense, there's nobody who works harder. Chris Benoit is just amazing. Even if you're not a fan of wrestling, if you see him in the ring, you have to do a double take and recognize there's something about him that's different than all the rest." In another interview, MVP called Benoit one of the five greatest wrestlers in history. "He's a machine. He's someone I've studied. . . . I'm a student of the game."

Likewise, Benoit was a follower of the sport. In a May 2007 interview with the British *Fighting Spirit Magazine*, he rhymed off many of the top stars not in WWE. "I've a lot of time for Bryan Danielson. And although I don't watch a lot of the TNA product, I've a lot of respect for Samoa Joe. Would I like to work with him? Sure — he's one of those guys I could fight a thousand times and we'd never have the same match. And, of course, there's Christopher Daniels and AJ Styles. I'd love to see AJ come to WWE just to give him the chance to be seen by the widest available audience — I'm a big, big AJ fan."

Shortly before his suicide, Benoit had been reassigned to the ECW brand. He was scheduled to face CM Punk for the ECW World title at the *Vengeance* pay-per-view in Houston. It was expected that Benoit would claim the belt and lead Punk to the next level of stardom in the process. "To better utilize his talent, because he was, across the board, probably the best wrestler in the WWE, and anyone would probably tell you that — so to move him to ECW was twofold," explained Chris Jericho on *Nancy Grace*. "One, he was about to become the ECW champion. And two, ECW is more with some younger guys that are just learning, and Chris was a great trainer and so well respected, they wanted him to be kind of more of a trainer to some of these younger guys to help them with their future endeavors. So to move Chris to ECW, Chris would not see that as a demotion. He would see it as doing his job, which is to help the business and to continue the business going, the business that he loved."

"I was always a huge fan of Chris Benoit and was extremely influenced by him and his work ethic," Punk told journalist Mike Mooneyham, explaining that he was flattered when he first met Benoit and that The Canadian Crippler knew all about Punk's career. "That paints a picture of who Chris Benoit was. He was a student of the game. He was a student when he really didn't need to be anymore."

Still to come in the future are Benoit's Calgary protégés Harry Smith, the son of "The British Bulldog" David Boy Smith; Nattie Neidhart, the daughter of Jim "The Anvil" Neidhart; and their childhood friend TJ Wilson. All three were nurtured by Benoit, who never missed a chance to sing their praises. "Harry Smith has just joined the WWE and, in my eyes, is going to be a huge part of the future of this industry," Benoit told a newspaper in England. "It's hard for me to talk about

31

him as one of the new guys as I've known him forever. Harry is so gifted as a wrestler — the best I've seen since I was a young man in Japan — and I have very high hopes for him." It was Benoit who lobbied for their hiring in WWE.

The irony is that the company where he found the most success, World Wrestling Entertainment, is doing its best to disassociate itself with Benoit and his legacy to the sport of professional wrestling. Footage of his matches has being taken out of DVD releases, his retrospective DVD *Hard Knocks* has been pulled from store shelves, past stories and interviews have been exorcised from its Web site, and in an extreme measure, his championship reigns have been removed from the official company line. On *Legends of Wrestling*, a round-table discussion show for the video-on-demand WWE 24/7 television service, the hosts somehow managed to talk about The Radicalz coming to the promotion without mentioning Benoit.

It's a sad testament to what was undoubtedly a Hall of Fame career. Future generations will never know what a great performer he was, and that's a shame. He epitomized what professional wrestling could and should be: hard-hitting, dramatic, serious action between high-caliber, exciting athletes.

"It's tarnished with this horrible, horrible tragedy. What sucks is that Chris will never go down in a Hall of Fame. He'll never from this point be remembered for being the wrestler that he was," said WWE tag champ Trevor Murdoch. "He's always going to be remembered for his last actions, his last three days. It's horrible that one man's life can be summed up in three

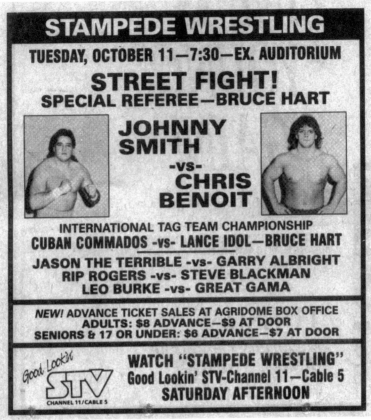

PHOTO: BOB LEONARD

days, but that's exactly what happened. It's human nature to remember the bad instead of the good."

Les Thatcher continues to have a photo of Daniel Benoit on his television set. The Benoits would send him an updated one every year. He has spent many sleepless nights dealing with what happened. "Did this happen? Yes. Is he guilty? Yes. Is it horrible? Yes. But he still has left a legacy in terms of what he did in-ring. And Nancy, the same way."

Jericho concurred: "We can also never forget or forgive these horrible acts. . . . And that overshadows everything else in his life. But you can't tell the story of pro wrestling without talking about Chris Benoit."

CHRIS BENOIT
TITLE HISTORY
Compiled by Greg Oliver

Stampede Wrestling (Western Canada)

International Tag Team Titles (4 times)

with Ben Bassarab

BEAT: "Honky Tonk" Wayne Farris & Ron Starr, March 1, 1986, in Regina, SK

LOST: Wayne Farris & Cuban Assassin (Angel Acevedo), March 21, 1986, in Calgary, AB

with Keith Hart

BEAT: Wayne Farris & Cuban Assassin, May 9, 1986, in Calgary, AB

LOST: Duke Myers & Kerry Brown, June 6, 1986

with Lance Idol

BEAT: Jerry Morrow & Cuban Assassin, October 7, 1988, in Calgary, AB

LOST: Jerry Morrow & Cuban Assassin, October 28, 1988, in Calgary, AB

with Biff Wellington (Shayne Bower)

BEAT: Makhan Singh (Mike Shaw) & Vokkan Singh (Gary Albright), April 8, 1989, in Calgary, AB

LOST: Bob Brown & Kerry Brown, June 9, 1989, in Calgary, AB

British Commonwealth Mid-Heavyweight Title (4 times)

BEAT: Gama Singh (Gadowar Singh Sahota), March 18, 1988, in Calgary, AB

LOST: Johnny Smith (John Hindley), June 10, 1988, in Calgary, AB

BEAT: Johnny Smith, June 17, 1988, in Calgary, AB

LOST: Johnny Smith, June 24, 1988, in Calgary, AB

BEAT: Johnny Smith, January 13, 1989, in Calgary, AB

LOST: Johnny Smith, July 7, 1989, in Dawson Creek, BC

BEAT: Johnny Smith, July 8, 1989, in Grande Prairie, AB

LOST: Gama Singh, August 4, 1989, in Calgary, AB

Universal Wrestling Association (Mexico)

WWF World Light Heavyweight Title

BEAT: Villano III (Arturo Díaz Mendoza), March 3, 1991, in Naucalpan, Mexico

LOST: Villano III, September 13, 1992, in El Toreo, Mexico

New Japan Pro Wrestling

IWGP Junior Heavyweight Title

BEAT: Jushin Liger (Keiichi Yamada), August 19, 1990, in Tokyo, Japan

LOST: Jushin Liger, November 1, 1990, in Tokyo, Japan

Super J Cup Tournament

1993 (Clinched June 14, in Osaka, Japan, beating El Samurai)

1994 (Clinched April 16, in Tokyo, Japan, beating Great Sasuke)

1995 (Clinched July 13, in Hiroshima, Japan, beating Shinjiro Otani)

Catch Wrestling Association (Germany)

CWA Tag Team Title

with David Taylor

BEAT: Franz Schumann & Miles Zrno, December 21, 1991, in Bremen, Germany

FORFEITED: June 1992, when Taylor is injured.

Extreme Championship Wrestling

ECW World Tag Team Title

with Dean Malenko (Dean Simon)

BEAT: Sabu (Terry Brunk) & Tazmaniac (Peter Senercia), February 25, 1995, in Philadelphia, PA

LOST: Public Enemy (Ted Petty & Mike Durham), April 8, 1995, in Philadelphia, PA (Triangle match also featuring Tazmaniac & Rick Steiner)

World Championship Wrestling

WCW TV Title (3 times)
BEAT: Booker T (Booker Huffman), April 30, 1998, in Augusta, GA
LOST: Booker T, May 1, 1998, in Greenville, SC

BEAT: Booker T, May 2, 1998, in Charleston, SC
LOST: Booker T, May 3, 1998, in Savannah, GA

BEAT: Rick Steiner (Rob Rechsteiner), September 13, 1999, in Chapel Hill, NC
LOST: Rick Steiner, October 24, 1999, in Las Vegas, NV

WCW World Tag Team Title (2 times)
with Dean Malenko
BEAT: Barry Windham & Curt Hennig, March 14, 1999, in Louisville, KY
LOST: Rey Misterio Jr. (Oscar Gutierrez) & Billy Kidman (Pete Gruner), March 29, 1999, in Toronto, ON

with Perry Saturn (Perry Satullo)
BEAT: Chris Kanyon (Chris Klucsarits) & Diamond Dallas Page (Page Falkinburg), June 10, 1999, in Syracuse, NY

LOST: Chris Kanyon & Diamond Dallas Page, June 13, 1999, in Baltimore, MD

United States Title (2 times)

BEAT: David Flair, August 9, 1999, in Boise, ID
LOST: Sid Vicious (Sid Eudy), September 12, 1999, in Winston-Salem, NC

BEAT: Jeff Jarrett, December 19, 1999, in Washington, DC (Ladder Match; Title was vacant)
LOST: Jeff Jarrett, December 20, 1999, in Baltimore, MD

WCW World Heavyweight Title

BEAT: Sid Vicious, January 16, 2000, in Cincinnati, OH (Title was vacant)
VACATED: January 17, 2000 (when Benoit jumped to WWF)

World Wrestling Federation / World Wrestling Entertainment

Intercontinental Title (4 times)

BEAT: Chris Jericho (Chris Irvine) & Kurt Angle, April 2, 2000, in Anaheim, CA (*WrestleMania XVI*)
LOST: Chris Jericho, May 2, 2000, in Richmond, VA

BEAT: Chris Jericho, May 8, 2000, in Uniondale, NY

LOST: Rikishi Phatu (Solofa Fatu, Jr.), June 20, 2000, in Memphis, TN

BEAT: Billy Gunn (Monty Sopp), December 10, 2000, in Birmingham, AL

LOST: Chris Jericho, January 21, 2001, in New Orleans, LA (Ladder Match)

BEAT: Rob Van Dam (Rob Szatkowski), July 29, 2002, in Greensboro, NC

LOST: Rob Van Dam, August 25, 2002, in Uniondale, NY

WWE Tag Team Titles (*Smackdown!*)
with Kurt Angle
BEAT: Edge (Adam Copeland) & Rey Mysterio, October 20, 2002, in Little Rock, AR (First champions after brand split)
LOST: Edge & Rey Mysterio, November 5, 2002, in Manchester, NH

World Tag Team Title (*Raw*) (3 times)
with Chris Jericho
BEAT: Triple H (Jean-Paul Levesque) & Steve Austin (Steve Williams), May 21, 2001, in San Jose, CA
LOST: The Dudley Boys (Mark LoMonaco & Devon Hughes), June 19, 2001, in Orlando, FL

with Edge
BEAT: Ric Flair & Dave Batista, April 19, 2004, in Calgary, AB

LOST: La Resistance (Sylvan Grenier & Rob Conway), May 21, 2004, in Montreal, QC

BEAT: La Resistance, October 19, 2004, in Milwaukee, WI

LOST: La Resistance, November 1, 2004, in Peoria, IL

United States Title (3 times)
BEAT: Orlando Jordan, August 21, 2005, in Washington, DC

LOST: Booker T, October 18, 2005, in Reno, NV

BEAT: Booker T, February 19, 2006, in Baltimore, MD

LOST: John Bradshaw Layfield, April 2, 2006, in Chicago, IL (*Wrestle-Mania 22*)

BEAT: Ken Kennedy (Ken Anderson), October 10, 2006, in Jacksonville, FL

LOST: Montel Vontavious Porter (Antonio Banks), May 20, 2007, in St. Louis, MO

World Heavyweight Title
BEAT: Triple H & Shawn Michaels (Michael Hickenbottom), March 14, 2004, in New York, NY (*WrestleMania XX*)

LOST: Randy Orton, August 14, 2004, in Toronto, ON

WE LOVED TO WATCH HER STRUT

WE LOVED TO WATCH HER STRUT

Greg Oliver

It was a different era.

To truly understand Nancy Toffoloni's impact on professional wrestling, you have to go back to 1984 and pretend to be, once again, a hormone-imbalanced teenager.

For decades, the women at the wrestling matches had been trainees of The Fabulous Moolah (Lilian Ellison). They wore full-body bathing suits and caked-on makeup, and there was a routine in their matches that aimed to prove that they belonged in the ring, the equal of the male wrestlers. If you were stimulated at all, that was a bonus; it certainly never seemed their intention. It was like watching your aunt wrestle.

But then came Kevin Sullivan and his crew of devil worshippers in *Championship Wrestling from Florida*. It was a daring angle for the time, with the "Prince of Darkness" spouting gibberish and perverting lesser minds. (Sullivan was careful never to use the word *devil* — it was the wrestling magazines that played up that aspect.)

More important to the male audience, however, was the woman at his side: Fallen Angel. Obedient and achingly sexy at Sullivan's feet, barely clad in a black bikini, with studded leather accessories, and often chained, Toffoloni was the one who really made the gimmick work. More than just the leather-fetish set were captivated.

"The beautiful, but vicious, Fallen Angel is a disciple of Kevin Sullivan, but no one can understand why the lovely lady is so taken by the crazed madman," wrote proficient photographer and scribbler George Napolitano at the time, crediting Fallen Angel's "exquisite looks" for defections into Sullivan's evil camp. Her beauty brought out an extra dimension in Sullivan's gimmick: that he was a master manipulator, with a mental control over those who followed him.

"It's a great relationship," Sullivan insisted to Napolitano. "She takes care of my needs in return for my spiritual guidance. I spoil her rotten, and I know I will never worry about someone else giving her flowers."

In one memorable television segment, Fallen Angel was instructed by Sullivan to shave one side of Luna Vachon's head. Sullivan was proud to create controversy. "[You're] gonna think while watching on TV something strange is going on, but you better go down to the arena to see what was going on," he said in 1994 in *The Pro Wrestling Torch*. "I was trying to draw money."

Away from Florida, Kevin and Nancy worked as hosts for National Wrestling Alliance's *Polynesian Pro Wrestling*, an hour-long show that was taped once a month in Knoxville, Tennessee, with producer Les Thatcher. It featured clips of matches from Hawaii and Southeastern Championship Wrestling. "They'd be in town for a couple of days, and Nancy would stay at my apartment on the couch. In the evenings, we'd just sit and chat, just became acquainted and became good friends," recalled Thatcher. The wraparounds [video segments] showed Nancy's comedic side, as she flirted with guest host celebrities or dressed up to play in *Miami Vice* skits.

The dark, occult-like storyline, which Sullivan kept up away from the arenas as well, wearing his black robe everywhere and traveling in a fiendishly decorated van, took a more personal twist when he (still married to his first wife, Jan) and Toffoloni fell in love. The relationship would seal her pact with the strange world of professional wrestling for evermore.

Paul and Maureen Toffoloni welcomed their daughter Nancy into the world on May 21, 1964, in Daytona Beach, Florida. Nancy would attend DeLand High School, and marry her sweetheart, Jim Daus, before school ended.

Two kids with little money, Jim and Nancy found entertainment in the weekly wrestling matches, often heading to Orlando to watch Florida stars such as Dusty Rhodes and Mike Graham from the front row.

Wrestling photographer Bill Otten, shooting at ringside in Orlando in late 1983, became captivated by Nancy's beauty, and she reminded him of the popular actress Valerie Bertinelli, who at the time was married to rock star Eddie Van Halen. Otten eventually convinced Nancy — who was answering phones for a local insurance agency — to give modeling a try. She posed for Otten with another bikini-clad girl in a shoot with the muscular Billy Jack Haynes; she also did a photo shoot of apartment wrestling, which was a common feature in the wrestling magazines of the time, a soft-core titillating series of shots where two women grappled wearing little clothing.

The pairing with Sullivan was in place by 1984, and they were married in 1985.

Demands of her wrestling schedule drove apart their marriage, said Daus. He suggested a divorce, and it was done quickly. "We cried a lot that day," Daus told ESPN.com. "It was very hard on me. That was the toughest year of my life, the year I got divorced."

Nancy really didn't know what she was getting involved with, content to ride out the wave. "I don't know what's going to happen. You never know what to expect," she told her hometown newspaper, the *Daytona Beach News-Journal*, in February 1986.

The Kevin Sullivan Satanic plot ran nearly three years in Florida, but the business changed during that period. The days of the small promotions were at an end; Jim Crockett Jr., the promoter in Charlotte, North Carolina, bought the

Florida company and rolled it into his expanding National Wrestling Alliance (later World Championship Wrestling). Sullivan was now both a wrestler and officially an assistant behind the scenes, writing storylines.

In 1989, Sullivan chose to put his wife, Nancy, onscreen again. Dressed down, with glasses and modest clothing, she was shown sitting ringside, cheering on brothers Rick and Scott Steiner. Rick Steiner (Rob Rechsteiner) portrayed a bit of a simpleton, and Nancy soon had him wrapped around her finger. Rick allowed her to come with him to the ring, where her true colors were revealed, and she cost Steiner his match.

Dropping the glasses, and dressing in sleek, form-fitting dresses, Nancy became a new character — Woman. Coming into the ring to Bob Seger's "Her Strut," she managed a masked team called Doom (Ron Simmons and Butch Reed), which debuted with a win over the Steiners at *Halloween Havoc '89* in Philadelphia.

Any past association with Sullivan was dismissed in the February 1990 edition of *The Wrestler*. "Doom is all I'm worrying about now. They are the most loyal, attentive men I've ever met," the "unscrupulous vixen," Woman, is quoted as saying.

When Doom broke up, she was placed in a short-lived angle with Ric Flair. She was pushing the idea of buying the Four Horsemen faction of star wrestlers, which Flair turned down on numerous occasions, but the angle hit a dead-end when the Sullivans left wcw in 1990.

The Sullivans would work many independent dates,

including significant time with the Savoldis' International Championship Wrestling promotion in the northeast and in Jim Cornette's Smoky Mountain Wrestling in the hills of Kentucky, where Nancy was known as Devil Angel.

In 1993, the Sullivans were together in the Philadelphia-based ECW for a short while, until Kevin left to return to WCW. Nancy stayed in ECW and was paired with The Sandman (Jim Fullington). It was her job to light the cigarettes and open the beer cans for the popular antihero. In ECW, she also managed 2 Cold Scorpio (Charles Scaggs).

"Me and Sandman were good, but Nancy taught us a lot and made us better," Scorpio said. "I mean, she learned the business from Sullivan, it's not like she was green."

When Nancy rejoined Kevin in WCW in 1995, their marriage was on the rocks. The pressure that Sullivan was under trying to book the chaotic WCW was immense, and he grabbed at every chance to create something successful. The oft-told tale of Sullivan booking his own divorce, pairing Nancy onscreen with Chris Benoit, which led to an offscreen relationship, is not exactly the way it happened. "She was a nice person. We just went our separate ways. She was nice and very loving," Sullivan told FOXNews.com after her death.

In WCW, Nancy was again known as Woman, and was used as a manager for the Four Horsemen, made up of Ric Flair, Arn Anderson, Chris Benoit, and Brian Pillman. When Pillman left the group, he would be replaced by Steve "Mongo" McMichael, who

Chris and Nancy in Calgary in May 1999. Left: Diana Hart Smith; rear: Rick
Titan and Chris Jericho.

brought his own eye candy, his wife, Debra, to the ringside.

Sullivan and Benoit began a heated feud, and Sullivan — ahead of the times as a scriptwriter — pushed the envelope of what was real and what was storyline. Benoit was shown dining with Woman in TV segments, and Benoit would refer to her as "Nancy." It was to play off the marriage problems that Kevin and Nancy Sullivan were suffering in real life.

The Sullivans divorced, and Benoit and Nancy became a couple. Yet, Kevin and Chris still had to compete in the ring. The awkwardness between the two would last for years, and Sullivan, being in a position of power, played a small role in Benoit's decision to leave WCW in 2000 for WWE.

When Sullivan lost a "retirement" match to Benoit in 1997, Nancy disappeared from television.

From all accounts, Nancy was content to fall into the role of a support person for Benoit, who she married in 2000. She would take care of her husband's business affairs from their home outside Atlanta. "I'm proud to know him, not just because I'm his wife, but because he's my best friend," she told the *Edmonton Sun* in May 2000. She made gift baskets as a hobby, earning some money on the side.

Nancy would give birth to the couple's son, Daniel Christopher, on February 23, 2000, by C-section. It was Benoit's third child; a son and a daughter from a previous relationship lived with their mother in Edmonton, Alberta.

Nancy rarely appeared publicly at wrestling events. Her most prominent moment came in March 2004, when she entered the ring with Daniel following Benoit's win of the WWE World title at *WrestleMania XX* held at New York's Madison Square Garden. Nancy was also at Benoit's side when he was honored as a homecoming champion in Edmonton later that same year.

A year earlier, in 2003, Nancy had filed a divorce petition, alleging "cruel treatment," but withdrew it a few months later. A request for a restraining order, in which she alleged that Benoit broke furniture and threatened her, was also dropped.

At Nancy's request, Benoit stayed home with his wife and son for four months in 2006, while she recuperated from neck surgery. In the spring of 2007, she accompanied her husband on a media tour of England.

The lives of Nancy and Daniel Benoit were remembered at a funeral service on July 14, 2007, at Our Lady of Lourdes Catholic Church in Daytona Beach. The media was not allowed into the church, and the family chose not to speak out. Fit Finlay was the only active WWE wrestler at the funeral, and WWE announcer Jim Ross spoke briefly with the media after the funeral.

"I've known Nancy for twenty years. She was always exuberant and fun to be around," Ross said. "Always laughing, had a great sense of humor. You know, was one of the guys. Had great timing in the ring, [and] was a beautiful lady."

STAMPEDE DAYS: A CRIPPLER ON THE RISE

STAMPEDE DAYS: A CRIPPLER ON THE RISE

Heath McCoy

Who was this little runt hanging around the Stampede Wrestling dressing room, and why the hell was The Dynamite Kid, the nastiest bastard on the circuit, actually being kind to him?

Bret Hart couldn't figure it out — he could hardly believe what he was seeing — but it was apparent even then that there was something special about this Chris Benoit kid.

It was at the Kinsmen Field House in Edmonton, recalls Bret, probably around 1980, that a young Benoit, awestruck and slightly terrified, was invited into the wrestlers' inner sanctum, if only for a moment, to meet his idol.

Bret is no longer certain who opened the door for the kid, though he guesses it was his father, Stu Hart, the rugged old dinosaur who ran Stampede Wrestling, a Calgary-based

Western Canadian institution that had been a beloved fixture of the region since the 1940s. Bret might have recognized the boy, vaguely. He was a devoted fan, present at the Edmonton matches every Saturday, studying the wrestlers' moves intently. He was so passionate, so dedicated that he stood out from your average fan, and that's why Stu would have rewarded him for his loyalty with a behind-the-scenes meet-and-greet.

But still, the way the wrestlers let their guard down ever so slightly when the kid came into the dressing room was virtually unheard of. It was almost as if, even then, they could sense he was one of them, a part of their blood fraternity.

"We all met him at the same time and we kind of dropped the kayfabe," says Bret. Pro wrestling is an illusion, a carnival-spawned act of sports theater with the wrestlers playing roles in the ring, enacting prearranged stories in a sort of two-fisted soap opera, and, in those days especially, it was the wrestlers' job to make the fans believe that the drama in the ring was real. That's what kayfabe was all about. You never let outsiders see those behind-the-curtain real-life aspects of the business. Never. If you got careless about this, Stu would growl, and nobody wanted that.

This scene with the Benoit boy then was a startling exception to the rule. Tom "The Dynamite Kid" Billington, about twenty-two at the time, was Stampede Wrestling's number-one heel, or villain. In keeping with kayfabe, he dwelled before and after every match in the heel dressing room, along with the other hated cheats, while Bret got ready for his matches in the babyface dressing room, where the rule-abiding good guys resided.

But for this meeting, Dynamite, who was then in the middle of a vicious feud with twenty-three-year-old Bret, stepped for a moment into the babyface dressing room.

"I distinctly remember him shaking The Dynamite Kid's hand," Bret says, "and Dynamite was really nice to him, which was strange. [Dynamite] was playing the role of the nasty punk-rock kind of heel and . . . he [wouldn't normally] break character to be nice to any kids. But he knew this kid really loved him, and he saw something in him. . . . Dynamite was a hard guy, it was tough to get his respect, and he always respected Chris."

Bret kept his distance while the meeting occurred, standing in the opposite corner of the room. By rights, Dynamite being in the same space with his hated rivals in the Hart family should have erupted into a chaotic brawl, so, for appearances, neither man was going to venture too close to the other, even though, when the fans weren't around, they were actually friends. A couple of years down the road they would be in-laws too, when they married two sisters. Back then all the Hart siblings treated Dynamite like one of their own, just as they would one day welcome Benoit into the fold.

From the short distance though, Bret could make out Benoit's conversation with Dynamite. He remembers the shy kid staring down at his feet, blushing, telling Dynamite how much he admired him, and that he one day hoped to follow in his footsteps.

It was unusual that a scoundrel such as Dynamite would have a fan who so obviously worshipped him. His job was to inspire hatred. Then again, Dynamite had a lot of admirers, though most of them were loath to admit it. That's because his wrestling style was so awe-inspiring — revolutionary in fact. Standing about five feet eight, and billed as being just over 200 pounds — though in reality he probably weighed closer to 180 before he eventually hulked out on steroids — the lean, muscle-ripped Kid was tiny next to the other wrestlers. Perhaps this struck a chord with Benoit, who was also a shrimp compared to most boys his age. Standing in that dressing room he was about thirteen years old, but Bret remembers him looking closer to nine or ten.

But despite his size, Dynamite stood out from his lumbering colleagues as the star of the show. Cocky and sneering, the little Englishman from the bleak coal mining town of Golborne in Lancashire would literally soar in that ring, launching into his opponents with flying head butts off the top turnbuckles. When shot off the ropes he was like a human rocket. He was unbelievably agile, flipping like an acrobat in and out of technical holds, dazzling his audience and his opponents alike. Dynamite was bloody tough too, his shots packing a sting that the whole audience could feel, his snap suplexes fast and mean when he brought his enemies crashing to the canvas on their backs. And boy, could he take a beating. When Dynamite was hit, he would shoot around the ring like a stone skipping across a pond. He made his opponents look like action heroes. That was the name of the game.

Decades later, when he himself had become a wrestling star, Benoit would still "mark out," gushing like a fan when talking about Dynamite Kid. "I looked up to him so much," he told this writer. "He was my Superman, my Batman, my Spider-Man, my comic-book superhero. His style was so aggressive and believable, so technically sound. Everything he did looked so snug. There was no wasted movement."

After Benoit had met Dynamite, he was ushered over to meet Bret, whom he also idolized. "He was so cute and lovable," Bret recalls. "He was adorable. He reminded me of my own little son when I look back at pictures."

That was a shocking way for Bret to describe Benoit in an interview conducted on June 26, 2007, the day after the grappler from Edmonton had been found dead in his home outside of Atlanta, along with the bodies of his wife, Nancy, and his seven-year-old son, Daniel. Police were saying that Benoit, forty, also known to the world as The Canadian Crippler and The Rabid Wolverine, had killed them over the weekend, strangling them before ending his own life by hanging himself on a weight pulley in his home gym.

But Bret's statement speaks volumes as to how highly Chris Benoit was regarded. From fans and the wrestling press to promoters and performers, nobody remotely familiar with the mat game could believe that Benoit would come to such a repellant, dishonorable, and utterly horrifying end.

Whether anybody wanted to admit it or not, the wrestling world had its share of short-fused gorillas, bullies, and steroid-stoked berserkers for whom such a destructive fate was at least conceivable. Even in the slick, orderly atmosphere of WWE — which prided itself in its corporate efficiency as respectable, if controversial, purveyors of sports entertainment — the business was still, at its core, a rough, knockabout world. Mean brutes with questionable values still roamed the playing field.

But Chris Benoit was never one of those guys. Or, at least, he never seemed to be. He was a soft-spoken gentleman, devoted to his family with a particular warm spot for children. He was a consummate professional who loved and respected the art of wrestling. He was a committed, hard-working athlete, a no-bullshit old-school grappler chiseled from that hard-man Stu Hart mold, who made it to the top by virtue of his toughness, talent, and tenacity. And he did so without any gimmicks or an obnoxious show-biz persona. He was a role model to the men in the locker room and a hero to fans around the world.

When people laughed at wrestling, dismissing it as idiotic fakery, when they turned up their nose at it for its descent into sleaziness, Benoit's was a name everybody could point to as an example of what was still good in the game. In and out of the ring, Benoit brought a sense of dignity and respectability to a business considered vulgar by most.

His tragic and shameful end was a devastating and demoralizing blow to the whole wrestling industry — and nowhere was that felt as profoundly as in Alberta. Benoit was a hometown boy who made his bones in the Hart's legendary Stampede Wrestling, back when Stu's wild cast of bruisers were folk heroes in the territory. Albertans were as proud of Benoit as they were of the Hart family themselves. Hell, when he came through Edmonton on April 18, 2004, after winning the WWE World Heavyweight title, the city's mayor declared a Chris Benoit Day. His disgrace was personally felt in this scrappy peacock of a province.

As for the Harts themselves, who had been pummeled by tragedies over the last decade — they were stricken by Benoit's disgraceful departure. He was, arguably, the greatest graduate from their father's notorious wrestler-spawning Dungeon, and, in many ways, they considered him one of their own. As far as the tight-knit wrestling fraternity went, he was certainly part of the Harts' inner circle. In many ways they considered him a brother, and another brother down was something this family could hardly bear.

At least from the time he was twelve, Chris Benoit was consumed with professional wrestling.

He was fairly new to Edmonton, a fresh transplant from Montreal, where he was born in 1967, when Bill Adomski began teaching him math and science at St. Edmund Junior High. Adomski also coached track and field at the school, and that's where Benoit distinguished himself. The boy excelled as an athlete, despite his size. "He was small in stature compared to the other kids," Adomski recalls, "he was only about five foot three in grade seven. But he was very tenacious in terms of athletics. His school work was okay . . . he was a good, average student . . . but school wasn't his priority. . . . He was a sprinter and very fast."

Adomski can still clearly remember Benoit's obsession with the mat game. "He was always talking about going to [Stampede Wrestling] matches . . . and even then I can remember him saying he wanted to be a wrestler. . . . He was focused on that dream."

In fact, one of Benoit's earliest memories was of the wrestling biz. He once told a Canadian Press reporter that he saw the legendary André The Giant wrestle in a Montreal handicap match when he was three years old.[1] Benoit was about twelve when his family moved to the Edmonton suburb of Sherwood Park and he began attending Stampede Wrestling matches. His imagination was captured.

"[Bret Hart] is another one that was such an influence on me," he said in 2004. "I remember going to the Kinsmen Field House and watching him wrestle Nick Bockwinkel [who was then the AWA World Heavyweight champion] in sixty-minute matches. Then I'd go to the concession stand afterwards, and Bret was there getting a hamburger. I remember standing behind him in line. It was so cool."

Vicki O'Neill taught Benoit grade eleven English at Archbishop O'Leary High School, where he played offensive end

---

1. Tara Brautigam, "After 20 years of broken teeth and bones, Chris Benoit is wrestling's top dog," *National Post*, April 15, 2004.

for the football team, and she too remembers the teen's passion for wrestling. "He was a really nice young man who was very committed to his vision," she recalls. "He knew exactly what he wanted to do. What was nice about Chris is we knew he wasn't interested in learning English, but he did the work. He came through and did what he had to do."

It seems that nearly everybody who knew Benoit as a young man tells a common story. He's almost always characterized as a polite, soft-spoken lad, a popular student from a friendly family who was wholly motivated by wrestling.

Being a regular at the Edmonton Stampede matches, Benoit eventually befriended a small group of like-minded kids. This group included Bob and Jeff Bulat, the sons of Mike Bulat, a high-school vice-principal. An associate of Stu Hart's since the 1950s, Bulat co-promoted Edmonton shows. Through the Bulats, Benoit met wrestler Mike Hammer, who hailed from St. Louis, Missouri. By no means a star, Hammer is described by those who knew him as a weird dude, remembered for his hard-living ways and a kinky penchant for sadomasochism. "He was just a jobber in the ring," says Stu's son, Ross Hart, "but actually, he was a fairly capable wrestler. Sometimes my dad wanted to put him over and he just didn't give a shit. . . . He was a little strange." For a time, Hammer took to training aspiring young wrestlers, including Benoit. "Mike taught him some basics," Ross says, "how to lock up, how to fall, things like that."

Even in those early days, Benoit had already begun taking steroids, according to wrestler Joe Zajko, who met Benoit when he was hanging around gyms in his mid-teens. Zajko says the youngster, who was self-conscious about his size and determined to break into the business, felt he had to take the drugs to be competitive.[2]

By the time Benoit graduated from high school an opportunity had arisen. In the summer of 1984, Stampede Wrestling shut down. Stu had sold his territory to Vince McMahon, head of the World Wrestling Federation, who was just beginning the aggressive expansion that would one day make him the kingpin of the wrestling business. The deal was that McMahon would pay Stu $1 million, with installments of $100,000 a year for ten years. But Alberta fans remained loyal to Stampede Wrestling, and initially they rejected WWF, whose shows did dismal business in the territory. After a year, McMahon told Stu he couldn't afford to pay him. Stu and Vince came to a revised agreement, which allowed Stampede Wrestling to begin anew. The problem was McMahon had recruited the territory's top draws — including Bret, Dynamite, and Davey Boy Smith — into the WWF. Stu's son Bruce Hart needed to train a new stable of wrestlers and he had a shortage of good-looking, talented babyfaces. For this, the Bulats recommended Benoit.

In the summer of 1985, Benoit made his first trip to the Hart house in Calgary, where the brothers were training wres-

---

2. Ryan Cormier and Elise Stolte, "Did steroids play a role? World Wrestling Entertainment says no; friends, fellow wrestlers raise the question," *Edmonton Journal*, June 27, 2007.

tlers in their basement gym, known as the Dungeon, and in their backyard wrestling ring, getting ready for the promotion's relaunch that October.

At that time, WWF's Hulk Hogan, a charismatic muscle-bound giant from Florida, was the biggest sensation in the wrestling world, and every territory was looking for their own replica. Bruce was grooming a pack of largely unpromising hulks — who thought that setting bench press records were more important than learning to wrestle — when Benoit arrived on the scene. The handsome young man had been training hard and already had the makings of a well-cut, solid frame, but the brutes towered over him. Even so, Benoit excelled while most of the others floundered. "He was a natural," says Ross. "He learned everything so fast. He was always patient and respectful, never a know-it-all. . . . He was willing to do whatever it took to break in."

Before long Benoit was a regular at the Hart house. He would work on the weekdays for his father's air-infiltration business, and every weekend he would catch the Greyhound to Calgary for another bout of punishing bumps and stretching in the Dungeon. A few times Stu himself came down to lock the kid up in his frighteningly painful, viselike holds. Benoit welcomed such torture as the powerful old man twisted his body into unnatural shapes until it seemed his neck might snap. "He was very willing to work out with Stu," Ross says. "That was his stamp of approval. He thought, 'I'm going to learn from this. This is what it takes to be accepted.'"

By the end of the year, Bruce determined that Benoit was ready for his debut. He moved to Calgary, staying in the attic of the elegant but filthy Hart mansion for a few weeks until he found a place to rent. Benoit began his career at the bottom of the Stampede cards, as the promotion toured the grueling prairie circuit seven days a week. But within a matter of months, his popularity and talent instigated a rise up the ranks. Soon he was made a champion, co-holding the Stampede International Tag Team title with Stu's son-in-law Ben Bassarab.

Over the duration of his Stampede tenure, where he wrestled off and on for close to four years, Benoit would also hold the tag team titles with Stu's son Keith and with a hard-living Calgary grappler who went by the name of Biff Wellington. As a singles competitor, Benoit would win the Stampede British Commonwealth Mid-Heavyweight title too, twice trading it back and forth with the devious Gama Singh and a tough young buck who wrestled as Johnny Smith, sold as a rogue cousin of Davey Boy Smith.

As far as Davey Boy himself went, when Benoit first showed up in the ring he wasn't welcomed by the beefy Brit. Davey Boy was still connected to Stampede, as he was married to Stu's daughter Diana, and he took exception to Benoit's appearance. "What the fuck is this guy doing here?" he demanded. "He hasn't paid any dues and now you're putting him on the card?"

On one hand, Davey Boy was being protective of the promotion, Ross says. "He thought Bruce was cutting corners just bringing this kid in." But Davey Boy also remembered Benoit as the ever-present Edmonton fan, and he held a grudge over it. "When Chris was a fan, he used to cheer on Dynamite, who was then a heel," Ross says. "Nothing pissed the baby-faces off more than someone who would heckle them or cheer the heels. . . . Davey was livid when he saw Chris."

Benoit's abilities quickly became apparent though, and soon Davey Boy — who was a star in the WWF working as part of a tag team called The British Bulldogs with his actual cousin, Dynamite Kid — welcomed Benoit into the fold. So did such seasoned veterans as Gama Singh, "Rotten" Ron Starr, Garry Morrow, The Cuban Assassin (Angel Acevedo), and the brutally tough, intensely scary "Bad News" Allen. This grizzly group could eat young wannabes alive if they chose. Countless green grapplers had been driven from the business over the decades, harshly schooled by old warhorses who wanted to keep the young, cocky, pretty boys in their place. Those were the politics of the game.

Notably, Brian Pillman, another future star who started in the promotion about a year after Benoit, was hated by many of his colleagues. A hot-tempered wild child and an incessant womanizer with an attitude who liked to shoot off his mouth, Pillman drew major heat from a number of the boys who were constantly grumbling about their intention to one day kick the shit out of him. And of course, Pillman was close friends with the boss's son Bruce, who many in the crew disrespected. In fact, Pillman rose to the top of the card as Bruce's partner in the tag team Badd Company. Because of this, some pegged Pillman as Bruce's stooge. But the truth was Pillman was a skillful, charismatic high-flyer. The fans loved him.

Though he was swimming in the same shark-infested waters as Pillman, Benoit never found himself in the same danger as Flyin' Brian, mainly because he possessed none of Pillman's arrogance. He kept his head down and his mouth shut in those politically volatile moments and focused on what mattered — his work. He didn't step on anybody's toes either. When he found himself in the ring with the veterans, he let them lead the match. He paid them respect, and they loved him for it.

Occasionally some bitter heel might try to screw him over in the ring, but when that happened, Benoit could take care of himself. The Harts looked out for him too. When Chris was tagging with Keith Hart, Ross remembers his older brother taking the kid under his wing. If anybody refused to cooperate with Benoit and sell his moves — acting like the fake blows were anything less than real — then Keith would step in and stretch them, landing a few real shots in the process. "We didn't want Chris getting that kind of treatment," Ross says. "This guy worked hard and he was no jobber."

Benoit proved night after night that he was every bit as impressive an athlete as Pillman, even if he lacked Brian's flair on the microphone. From his earliest days in the ring, Benoit's own high-flying, hard-hitting style was reminiscent of that of his childhood idol. Bret Hart once commented that he saw "the ghost of The Dynamite Kid" when he watched Benoit work.

It's grimly ironic now, but in his prime those who pointed out the similarities between Benoit and Dynamite always stressed the same differences: Dynamite was a self-destructive, hard-partying devil with a mean streak. Benoit was even-tempered, level-headed, and moderate in his excesses. Wrestler Mike Shaw, who was better known as Karachi Vice villain Makhan Singh, described Benoit as "Dynamite without the dark side," a mere three years before The Canadian Crippler's demise.

Benoit appeared a gentleman even when it came to women, which wasn't a common trait among many of the Stampede stars in those days. "Unlike a lot of the wrestlers who cheated on their wives and their girlfriends . . . I never saw Chris try to pick up ring rats [the wrestling equivalent of the groupie]," Ross says. "One girl he used to [date], you wouldn't see her at the matches very often. She was very quiet and reserved, not too vocal or opinionated like some of the damsels who would come to the shows. . . . A lot of the guys cared more about getting pussy after the matches. Chris was focused on the wrestling and his training. He'd get up early, wherever we were, and have a two-hour workout. He was careful about what he was eating. He was very straight, never smoked, seldom did I see him drinking."

But even if recreational drugs weren't his thing, Benoit was indulging heavily in steroids. When Benoit was teamed up with Biff Wellington the two friends became known among the boys for their prodigious intake on the road. "At one point we called them The Mega-Doses," says Milad Elzein, who played the role of Abu Wizal, the crooked Arab manager of Karachi Vice. "That's because they were taking such big doses of steroids."

"I never saw him shooting steroids . . . but I'm not under any illusions," Ross says. "It was pretty obvious seeing his muscularity . . . and how fast he developed. . . . I think there was a lot of exposure to it, being around guys like Dynamite, Davey Boy, and Pillman. So many of the guys were taking major 'roids . . . . Chris was doing it to enhance his performance."

Throughout his incredible career, Chris Benoit accumulated countless treasures, including, of course, the top prize in the sport, the WWE World Heavyweight title. But a month after he won that championship in 2004, when he was asked about Dynamite Kid's boots, he still considered them among his greatest trophies. They sat in a place of honor in his home office in Atlanta, along with his other mementos. "I value them so much," he said, his eyes glittering.

Sometime in 1989, in Stampede Wrestling, a drunken Dynamite, who had been indulging in the dressing room, staggered to the ring after one of Benoit's matches and presented the young man, then only twenty-two, with a pair of his boots. Dynamite hung them around Benoit's neck and shoulders in what was clearly a sentimental and symbolic gesture. He was passing the torch by handing his boots to the only wrestler he considered fit to wear them.

While only thirty years old himself, the great Dynamite Kid was on his way down in the world, and in the back of his bruised, angry mind he knew it. Years of steroid abuse and hard, decadent living, combined with a dangerous, punishing style in the ring, had broken Tom Billington. His body was failing him, and before his fortieth birthday he would find himself confined to a wheelchair. Meanwhile, his malicious behavior — pulling twisted, hurtful pranks, and acting like a bullying tyrant in the dressing room — had also burned a major bridge for Dynamite when he left WWF on bad terms, after getting his teeth knocked out backstage by wrestler Jacques Rougeau. The French Canadian star, who was brandishing a roll of quarters when he delivered the blow, was retaliating for a beating Dynamite had laid on him previously, sucker punching him in the dressing room for some perceived insult.

The British Bulldogs left WWF and returned to Stampede Wrestling at the tail end of 1988. Those close to the prideful Dynamite say he was never able to psychologically get over the beating Rougeau gave him, which made him more fierce and volatile than ever. As for his demented sense of humor, it had never been more malignant.

Dynamite was fond of stealing wrestlers' bags before they were off to the next city, or maybe taking scissors and cutting up their clothes. Taking off in the van in the midst of a road trip, stranding some poor sap in the middle of nowhere on a frozen prairie highway, was another trick. Drugging his colleagues and humiliating them, perhaps shaving their heads, was a grand gag. And then there was his specialty, spiking some unwitting grappler's drink with enough laxatives that he shit himself in the ring and suffered horrible stomach cramps for days to come.

God help those for whom the Bulldogs had a hate-on. Dynamite resented Pillman and was constantly out to make his life hell, though Brian was somewhat protected by the Harts. But being a Hart didn't help Bruce when Dynamite attacked him one night at a show in the Northwest Territories and led a full-on violent mutiny against Stu's son.

Somehow though, Benoit always had Dynamite's admiration. "Dynamite shit on a lot of guys, but he always liked Chris very much," Ross says. "That's respect Chris earned. . . . He had fire and timing and he was never greedy in the ring."

Still, even Benoit found his initiation into the business via Stampede Wrestling a trial by fire. While craziness always reigned behind the scenes in Stampede, the late 1980s saw that chaos hit a fever pitch, with the majority of the crew stoked mad on everything from steroids to cocaine. This was a vicious gang to roll with.

When Benoit was asked about those days in 2004, he painted a vivid picture. "Every week ten or twelve of us would be packed into a van and driving from Calgary [all across the prairies]," he recalled. "We had to entertain ourselves. Usually the weak one in the herd would get picked and the rest of the hyenas would jump on him, start ripping at him and tearing him apart until he snapped and cracked. . . . I saw them drive Bill Kazmaier crazy, and at that time he was the strongest man in the world. He could wrap his hands around your neck and literally kill you. They drove him nuts. I've seen him totally lose it. If you showed any weakness, they picked you apart. . . . I was lucky. I got along with everyone, even the heavy ribbers.

"[But] you travel around the world and talk to guys from other territories and they all know [that] Stu Hart's Stampede territory had that reputation. Guys up there would rip the hell out of you and drive you out of town. It had that reputation throughout the wrestling world of being the wild west of territories."

Somehow Benoit managed to walk a fine line. He was one of the boys without sinking to their depths of depravity. Ross only ever saw him get carried away once when a young wrestler was showing disrespect to the older grapplers. "He was telling a lot of these guys he was a shooter and he could kick their asses," Ross says. "I was driving the van and Chris got up from the second [row of] seats, grabbed [the kid] by his collar and tried to choke him out. . . . I said 'Chris, cool it! I'm driving here. We're going to have an accident.' That was the only time I ever saw him riled."

Some Stampede wrestlers from Benoit's era feel that, despite his talent and popularity with the fans, he was never given the push he deserved in the territory. The undisputed babyface star of the promotion in the late 1980s was Stu's youngest son, Owen Hart, who started his career a few months after Benoit and was immediately rocketed into the main event.

Many of the old boys argue that Benoit was just as gifted as the fair-haired Hart and that Owen's preeminence on the card was yet another case of the Harts out to make stars of their own. This is not fair to Owen, an amazing talent who combined soaring aerial moves with a sound technical style. And unlike the reserved Benoit, Owen took to the theatrical aspect of the biz easily. He was a charismatic, natural performer almost from the moment announcer Ed Whalen stuck the microphone in his face. Nevertheless, it's a common complaint among the old guard that Stampede was a tough territory to work in if you were a babyface, because you always wound up in the shadow of a Hart, and Benoit often lived in Owen's.

The cantankerous "Bad News" Allen, who was frequently at odds with the Harts, took a special interest in Benoit, and in late 1986 he got the up-and-comer booked in Japan, where News himself broke into the business. The Harts were less than thrilled with this, as Benoit was one of their best workers, but News convinced the lad, with some validation, that this was a great opportunity.

The New Japan promotion billed Benoit as Dynamite Chris — because of his similarities to Tom Billington — and featured him in preliminary bouts. They also beat the hell out of the young Stampede star. It was their way of separating the strong from the weak, but some of the tests were sadistic. Benoit recalled an incident where one wrestler after another would punch him in his ears until they bled, yet he was always willing to submit himself to such torture if that's what it took to make it.[3] For the remainder of his Stampede tenure, Benoit would often travel back and forth to Japan.

By 1989, the foundations of Stampede Wrestling were crumbling. Despite the reputation it had established all over the world, Stu Hart's homegrown operation could simply not compete with the glitzy big-budget standards that Vince McMahon had established. Compared to the media colossus that was the WWF, Stampede looked increasingly like a ramshackle backwater promotion, especially since it was continually losing its best talent, with the likes of Pillman, "Bad News," and even Owen leaving for more lucrative pastures. Attendance was dropping across the touring circuit too. Fans were no longer willing to pay to see Stampede matches each week when the world's biggest wrestling stars could be seen year round on WWF's many TV programs and special event pay-per-views. Stu Hart was losing thousands of dollars each week.

Many valiant attempts were made to keep the Stampede tradition alive. One angle that was hugely promising involved the breakup of the British Bulldogs, who were renowned all over the world. Benoit was incorporated into this storyline, joining the heroic Davey Boy Smith as he went to war with his former partner, the evil Dynamite Kid, who was partnered with Johnny Smith. But several factors derailed the Battle of the Bulldogs,

---

3. David Meltzer, *Wrestling Observer Newsletter*, July 2, 2007.

including Dynamite's health problems and his deteriorating relationship with the Harts.

Then there was the ugly crackup in July 1989 when, as Benoit and the boys were traveling to a match in Jasper, Alberta, Ross lost control of the van on a patch of ice while negotiating a sharp curve. For one terrifying instant, the wrestlers thought they were done for as the skidding van was headed for a plunge off the mountain. Instead, they smashed into an oncoming station wagon.

Benoit was sitting behind Ross, and on impact he came crashing towards the front seat. Ross instinctively stuck out his arm to prevent the rookie from flying out of the van. "I swear to this day that was the only thing that stopped Chris from going through [the windshield]," Ross says. Benoit came out of the collision with a minor knee injury, which caused him to sit out of work for about three weeks. Davey Boy wasn't so lucky. His head smashed through the windshield, and not only did he take 135 stitches to the brow, he also suffered two herniated discs at the top of his spine. He was out of the game for five months, and the warring Bulldogs angle was sunk.

So was Stampede Wrestling. By January 1990 the legendary promotion officially closed down. A couple of short-lived independent promotions rose up in the months that followed Stampede's demise to try and fill the void, but Benoit distanced himself from them. Instead, he headed back to Japan. Ross explains: "After Stampede was over, that's where he wanted his career here to end."

Breaking a talent such as Chris Benoit into the business had always been a source of pride for the Harts, and it swelled to tremendous proportions as his reputation grew in the 1990s. By the tail end of the decade, wrestling aficionados viewed Benoit as one of the purest, most cutting-edge athletes in the game and his glory was, in a sense, the Harts' glory.

When they'd run down the stunning list of greats that had either graduated from their family promotion, or from their father's Dungeon, Benoit's name was at the forefront, alongside the likes of Fritz Von Erich, "Superstar" Billy Graham, Archie "The Stomper" Gouldie, Greg "The Hammer" Valentine, The British Bulldogs, Chris Jericho, and, of course, Bret and Owen Hart. Benoit's legend was one of the strongest testaments to the Hart family's enormous impact on the wrestling world.

His accomplishments were stellar. As it turned out, establishing himself in New Japan was one of the best moves of Benoit's career, no matter how long it took him to rise through the ranks. After Stampede ended, New Japan reinvented Benoit as a masked wrestler called Pegasus Kid, a gimmick he took with him on tours through Mexico and Europe. His gripping matches during this time put Benoit on the world map, and, as he mastered every foreign style he encountered, industry insiders came to regard him as, pound-for-pound, one of the best wrestlers in the business.

While touring through Germany, Benoit met his first wife, Martina, eventually bringing her back to Alberta, where they

PHOTO: MIKE LANO

Benoit with Tito Santana and 2 Cold Scorpio in ECW.

raised two children together. But Benoit never lost his focus on
his first love: wrestling. In North America he dropped the Pegasus gimmick, eventually appearing as The Canadian Crippler
when he wrestled for the hard-core promotion ECW in 1994,
before signing on with Ted Turner's WCW in 1995.

Even though his work was second to none, Benoit was
seldom allowed to rise beyond the rank of a mid-card performer due to WCW's infamous backstage politics and senseless
booking strategies. He had a few moments of glory in the
promotion, including a fleeting instant where he held the
WCW World Heavyweight Championship, but for the most
part Benoit's time there was frustrating. He did however meet
his second wife in the promotion, in what was to ultimately
prove a tragically fateful twist.

Nancy Toffoloni was a gorgeous brunette from Florida with a sultry air and a gleam in her eye that made her look something like Valerie Bertinelli's long-lost bad girl of a sister. She had been involved in wrestling since the mid-1980s when she began appearing as the beautiful, and, at times, Satanic valet known as Fallen Angel, who would accompany her then husband, Kevin Sullivan, to the ring.

In 1996, Sullivan, who was both wrestling and working as a booker for wcw, conceived an angle in which Benoit was having an affair with his wife. This blew up in Sullivan's face when the make-believe tryst turned real, and Benoit and Nancy became an item. The two eventually married in 2000 around the time Nancy gave birth to their son, Daniel.

Benoit was stifled more often than not in wcw, and it's somehow fitting that one of his biggest breaks there came courtesy of a Hart. Bret Hart joined the company in 1997, after an infamously bitter split with wwf that same year. Bret's acrimony with the company was tragically intensified when Owen Hart died in a wwf wrestling ring in Kansas City on May 23, 1999, after an ill-advised stunt went awry. Owen was being lowered into the ring from the rafters of the arena when his safety harness released prematurely, causing him to plunge to his death. Owen's wife, Martha, and his parents, Stu and Helen, launched a civil suit against McMahon and others for wrongful death due to negligence. The Harts later received U.S.$18 million in a settlement and, years later, Bret and McMahon even mended fences.

But on October 4, 1999, the wrestling world was reeling from this disaster and all eyes were on Bret when wcw came to Kemper Arena, where Owen had died less than five months before. For the show, Bret planned to wrestle in a main-event tribute match to his youngest brother, and he handpicked the Hart family's esteemed friend Benoit as his opponent.

"I rode with Chris and Owen a few times and I remember they were so close," Bret says. "I don't think anybody took Owen's death harder than Chris. Of course, the family did, but I think Chris was a part of our family when all that happened. . . . There was only one guy that I felt could honor Owen in this match and that was Benoit. . . .

"Me and Chris made a specific attempt to give [the fans] an old-school match with holds and a great storyline, just to show you didn't need to drop from the ceiling to have a good match. You didn't need to set each other on fire. We just went out there and worked. It was hard for the first couple of minutes. People were scratching their heads because they don't see that anymore. But by about the fifteen-minute mark, the place was going crazy."

It was the highest profile U.S. match of Benoit's career at that point and in it he shined, proving his worth once and for all. Still, wcw never quite seemed to get it, and in 2000 Benoit jumped from that sinking ship over to wwf.

Even there it seemed that at times Benoit did not rise as fast as his talent would warrant. Despite the massive, ripped build that years of hard-core training and steroids had given him, he was still a relatively small man in a world where monsters dominated the main event. And even though his promo skills had improved over the years, he still came off as a strong silent type in a world where a charismatic loud-mouth always had a leg up. The fact that he was sidelined for a year in 2001 — after shattering two discs in his neck, which forced him to undergo neck fusion surgery — also represented a significant road block.

Nevertheless, Benoit made a huge comeback, and by the time *WrestleMania XX* rolled around in March 2004 — when he won the WWE World Heavyweight Championship by forcing Triple H to tap out in the grip of his signature submission hold, the Crippler Crossface — it was hard for anybody to deny. Chris Benoit was the greatest wrestler of his day — maybe one of the greatest ever.

As he rose to the top of his profession, some of Benoit's old friends from his Stampede days felt that he turned his back on them. Former tag team partners such as Ben Bassarab and Biff Wellington were resentful, and even "Bad News" Allen, who had gotten Benoit booked in Japan, felt forsaken. "He was a good kid at the time," News huffed in a 2004 interview. "Now you can't get him to return a phone call."

But Benoit certainly never forgot the Harts. Their legend was at the very root of his own after all, and Benoit frequently spoke of them with reverence. He paid his respects to the family as often as he could. When the Harts organized a one-off show in 1995 in honor of Stu's eightieth birthday, Benoit made

sure he was there. In 2001, when WWE came to Calgary's Sad-
dledome for a televised match, Benoit and Jericho stood in
the ring and paid an emotional tribute to Stu, who was in
attendance, for the entire world to see.

And as the Harts fell victim to one tragedy after another,
Benoit was there for them. When Owen died in 1999, he was
on hand to grieve with the family. He found himself in Calgary
again when Davey Boy Smith passed away from a heart attack
in 2002 at the age of thirty-nine, after years of steroid and drug
abuse. When Stu died the following year, it's doubtful anything
could have kept Benoit away.

When the horrific news about the death of the Benoit family
broke from Atlanta on June 25, 2007, the world was aghast.
Once the details of the incident became clearer in the days that
followed, and it was evident that this was a case of murder-
suicide perpetrated by Chris, the entire wrestling community
was deeply troubled.

The pain and shame in Alberta — where Benoit's roots
were still firmly entrenched — was particularly acute. From
his family and his friends to the fans and his brothers in the
Stampede Wrestling fraternity, everybody struggled to accept
this tragedy. Nobody seemed entirely able to reconcile the hon-
orable Benoit they knew with the monster he somehow became
behind closed doors.

"It knocked you off your feet the second you heard it,"
said the retired Bret Hart, who soon found himself discuss-

ing the scandal on such international programs as *Larry King Live* and *Nancy Grace*. "I haven't pulled myself up yet. I can't even understand it. . . . I refuse to believe anything of this nature until I hear the final version. I can't imagine Chris killing his son. I'm going to wait for a better verdict than that."

Ross Hart was equally unwilling to believe the worst about his friend. "This would be very uncharacteristic of Chris to do anything self-destructive. I find it very hard to believe that he would end his life or his family's. I have to expect foul play." Ross added, sadly: "[This] is really the most significant loss [to the wrestling world] since my brother Owen died. [Benoit] was a hallmark of our promotion and such an international star. It's a huge blow to the whole industry and very much felt by our family."

"This almost stops me cold," said Bob Leonard, a photographer and promoter for Stampede Wrestling for decades. "When I look at all the people I've known in fifty years in this business, I would say Chris would be one of the most stable people I've ever seen. . . . I think there's a lot more to be learned here about what the circumstances were. Something must have driven him to that . . . because he was a very controlled, focused guy."

Benoit's immediate family, for the most part, refused to talk to the swarming press. When Chris's first wife, Martina, was contacted by a reporter, she said her ex-husband "was the most loving person anyone could imagine." She lashed out at media reports on his death as "crap," before hanging up the phone.[4]

His father, Michael, told one reporter that he had last spoken to his son on Father's Day, at which time Chris expressed his regrets that he had to work that day and couldn't spend it with his family. "That really wouldn't give you an indication of someone who would do what he did a week later," Michael said. "We have no understanding of why this happened."[5]

Many of Benoit's WWE colleagues remembered him as a devoted, loving family man, a guy that would fly home whenever possible after a show to see his wife and child, even if only for a few hours, when it would have been easier to stay on the tour and go straight to the next gig.

Up-and-coming wrestler Nattie Neidhart — daughter of Jim "The Anvil" Neidhart and a granddaughter of Stu Hart — was living in Atlanta in the months leading up to the tragedy, training in WWE's developmental camp, and she grew close to the Benoit family and was invited to their home on several occasions. As a final show of devotion to the Hart family, Benoit was trying to use his influence to get Nattie a place on the WWE roster, along with Stu's other grandchildren Teddy Hart and Harry Smith (son of Davey Boy Smith). "He was almost

---

4. Kevin Duffy, "Benoit 'loving person,' ex-wife says," *Atlanta Journal-Constitution*, June 28, 2007.

5. Ajay Bhardwaj, "'We'll have to live with this' Anguished family seeking clues to Chris Benoit's murderous rampage," *Edmonton Sun*, June 30, 2007.

their guiding light down there," Bret says. "They became his personal project."

WWE would not permit Nattie to give interviews after the incident occurred, but according to her uncles, she came away from the Benoit home believing they were a happy family. "Nattie described how [Daniel] worshipped Chris, had all his action figures, and Chris would play games with him when he came home," Ross says. "And Nancy was a very devoted mother."

As the story progressed though, a darker side of the Benoit family emerged. Though they put on a happy front for almost everybody around them, it seemed Chris and Nancy had a volatile relationship, marked by at least one incident of domestic abuse, according to a court petition filed by Nancy. It was believed that the couple fought in recent years over the care of Daniel, who was said to have had a learning disability, possibly even Fragile X syndrome, a mental impairment often accompanied by autism.

It also came to light that Benoit suffered from severe depression over the deaths of many of his wrestling colleagues, most notably his best friend Eddie Guerrero in 2005. Benoit had been living on a diet of steroids and painkillers for years, and his intake spiraled out of control as his despair grew, with anti-depressants added to the menu. Nancy told her closest friends that Benoit had begun to show chilling signs of paranoia.[6]

6. David Meltzer, *Wrestling Observer Newsletter*, July 2, 2007.

Steroids and a variety of prescription drugs were found in the Benoit home after the murders, and Georgia's chief medical examiner later determined that the wrestler's body contained ten times the normal levels of testosterone when he died. Benoit was full of steroids when he committed the murders. But despite all the hysteria about "roid rage" heard in the media, the medical examiner said there was not sufficient proof that his actions were the result of an uncontrollable fury. In fact, there was much about the incident that indicated deliberation, not rage. Still, years of steroid and prescription drug abuse may well have played a part in Benoit's personal descent.

Even before the medical examiner's findings, Bruce Hart condemned Benoit in the media calling him a "delusional juice freak" and adding: "The last time I saw him he was in pretty rough shape mentally." [7]

Meanwhile, in a disturbing coincidence, news circulated around Calgary that Benoit's former Stampede tag team partner Biff Wellington, born Shayne Bower, had died at the age of forty-four, around the same time as his former friend. His heart failure was attributed to years of drug abuse.

Looking back at the Stampede crew during Benoit's days in the promotion, former heel manager Milad Elzein was dismayed to report that "of the fourteen guys we used to travel

---

7. Steve Simmons, "'Freak' Wrestling legend says Benoit had trouble with reality," *Toronto Sun*, June 29, 2007.

with . . . eight of them are dead right now." And while a few of those deaths — like Owen Hart and "Bad News" Allen — were unrelated to routine steroid and drug abuse, so many of them could be linked to those landmines, including "Lethal" Larry Cameron, Davey Boy, and Brian Pillman. The phenomenon was by no means exclusive to Stampede Wrestling. Since 1999, a long list of major stars of the industry have died similar deaths, several of them Benoit's friends.

It's not difficult to understand how so many wrestlers became drug dependent. Considering the severity of the neck injury that almost ended his career in 2001, one has to guess that Benoit wrestled in an enormous amount of agony. When asked about the injury in 2004 he replied: "Me being who I am, I thought 'I'm going to work through this,' I just kept pushing myself and it just kept getting worse and inevitably, I was in chronic pain. I had to accept the fact that I was injured, which was hard. . . . There's a lot of pride that goes into what we do and a lot of wrestlers have that mentality. We're on the road year round, and it's hard to step back and say 'Hey, look, I need some time off.' . . . I grew up as a kid watching Stampede Wrestling and wanting to become this and now that I am, I feel very gifted. I feel blessed to have this opportunity, and I never want to take advantage of it."

In hindsight, those words seem so telling now. That he was also reportedly paranoid about his position in WWE brings us an even greater understanding as to how Benoit fell victim to that vicious cycle of painkillers and performance-enhancing drugs that, over time, may have contributed to his becoming so deranged.

Ultimately, Bret believes, the world will never fully understand what was going on in Benoit's head when he committed his hideous deeds. "Something must have snapped in him somewhere," he says. "There's no explaining this anymore than you can explain Columbine or any of those horrible things where people lose it."

Bill Adomski, Benoit's former teacher, agrees. Adomski knew Benoit as a good, humble man who never forgot his Alberta roots, and he was shocked by his famed student's fall from grace. "There must have been a certain point in his life where, for that one split second he did the wrong thing and it got away from him," Adomski says. "Unfortunately, with this one, the results were tragic."

With all the friends he had, it's heartbreaking that Benoit never confided in any one when he was clearly going through such an emotional crisis. But then again, silently suffering was in keeping with his personality. Benoit prided himself on being strong — old-school, Stu Hart strong — and crying on a friend's shoulder, admitting to any sort of pain, was not something he could easily do. "It was his quiet nature that he didn't reach out to a lot of guys," Ross says. "He was reserved, very discreet. Maybe there was a side of him we didn't know."

Like so many around the world, Ross feels angry at Benoit — and betrayed by him. "It's a horrible thing he's done, and it ruined his legacy," Ross says.

If the Chris Benoit that people knew and loved could have seen into his future — if he could have caught a glimpse of his nightmarish fate and its aftermath — two things might have torn his heart apart, killing him on the spot. One of them, of course, would be the sheer horror that his beloved family would die by his own hands. But, as Bret believes, the other thing that would have eaten Benoit alive was that his act would cause such damage and pain to the wrestling community. "He was a guy that absolutely loved wrestling," Bret says. "He loved everything about it." Chris Benoit spent his life striving to elevate the wrestling business with his incredible work in the ring. That he ultimately did so much to drag it down and scandalize it in the eyes of the public would have shamed him to the core.

'ROIDS, REPORTERS, AND RASSLIN': ANATOMY OF A FEEDING FRENZY

'ROIDS, REPORTERS, AND RASSLIN': ANATOMY OF A FEEDING FRENZY

Steven Johnson

On a December day in 2005, Dave Meltzer, editor of the *Wrestling Observer Newsletter*, which is to wrestling what *Variety* is to the entertainment industry, was on the phone with a former WWE world champion when the toxicology report on Eddie Guerrero's death was released. The conclusion was expected — the Latino star had died a few weeks before at age thirty-eight, his enlarged heart irreparably damaged by years of steroid and substance abuse. This was it, Meltzer and the wrestling star agreed. The press had been harping on steroids in athletics; Congress hauled in the heads of major sports leagues for questioning about the effectiveness of their drug-testing policies. Now the media had its smoking gun. "He said it first, 'Oh, my god, this is going to be gigantic!'" Meltzer said. "I go, 'I know. Every baseball writer in the country has their steroid victim.' We expected it to be huge news the next day and it wasn't news at all. I mean, nobody even picked up on it. And here you had a guy that died. It was steroids and growth hormone right across the board. Eddie was on those Latino TV commercials and was really at his peak as a personality. It was like a nonstory." In fact, *The New York Times* expended 470 words on Guerrero in two short stories. In the *Los Angeles Times*, Guerrero merited a forty-one-word obituary. WWE chairman Vince McMahon appeared on the *Rita Cosby: Live & Direct* show on MSNBC to pay quiet tribute to Guerrero. Meltzer, who has chronicled how the premature death rate of wrestlers rivals that of postwar navy test pilots, arrived at a sad conclusion. "My thought was, 'Okay, now I know. I don't care if there's two hundred people that died — this will never become a story. You will never have a bigger star than Eddie Guerrero die with steroids right on his death certificate. It will never happen again.'"

For decades, the press has treated professional wrestling like a crazy uncle, amusing in a quirky sort of way but, for the most part, better off tucked away safely in the attic, brought into plain sight only on special occasions. Dan Parker spent a good part of his thirty-eight years as a columnist for the *New York Daily Mirror* deriding and ridiculing wrestling to the point of disclosing outcomes days before bouts took place. After the Second World War, *The New York Times* took a tongue-in-cheek tack of reporting matches in the manner of a Broadway play.

Gordon S. White Jr., a veteran sportswriter at the paper, recalled the farcical treatment served up by colleague Joe Nichols. "He pulled a gag that was accepted and was absolutely perfect. He wrote it up as if it was a theater event. He's the first one to have done this. If you notice the theater review pages, you always have a little box at the top of the story that gives the name of the play, the producer, and then the cast. He would put down 'Wrestling at the Garden' produced by whomever, then below he would put down 'Good guy . . . Antonino Rocca,' 'Bad guy . . . Gorgeous George.'"

In the ensuing years, wrestling suffered its share of black eyes in the press. A 1991 steroid and drug scandal involving a former ringside physician led to the indictment of McMahon on steroid-related charges; he was acquitted in 1994. In May 1999, Owen Hart plunged to his death during a pay-per-view stunt that went awry; a few voices called for industry reform but soon faded. Mostly, what coverage there was centered on the outrageous nature of the business, such as the stories that accompanied a spring 2007 "shave your head" challenge between McMahon and tycoon Donald Trump.

The revelation that Chris Benoit murdered his wife, Nancy, and son Daniel before taking his own life at his Atlanta-area house in late June 2007 challenged the media's view of wrestling like never before. "My first surprise was that they paid any attention to it because it was a pro wrestler. It's that stigma that's been about wrestling from the beginning," said Paul MacArthur, a public relations professor at Utica

College and co-publisher and co-editor of *Wrestling Perspective* newsletter. "I think a lot of these media outlets did not want to do the story." Case in point — CNN's *Anderson Cooper 360°* ignored the incident on June 25, the day the news of the murders broke, then offered a short exchange the next night with wrestler Brian Christopher (Brian Lawler), who lacked any discernable connection to Benoit, the victims, or the current wrestling scene. "You know, we generally don't do sports stories here at *360°*. And that's why, when we first heard yesterday about a pro wrestler and his family found dead, we decided we wouldn't cover it," Cooper explained.

But the staggering level of public interest, especially in the wired world, was hard to ignore. At the SLAM! Wrestling Web site, page views of a vanilla biography of Benoit, which averaged thirty to sixty per day before the murders, soared to 43,000 on June 25, the first day of the story, and 93,000 the next day. According to The Lycos 50, a popular Web keyword count, searches for Benoit skyrocketed 3,638 percent in the first forty-eight hours after the murders became known, and search interest in Benoit was 1,518 percent more popular than searches for McMahon. That told the media something — curiosity extended beyond hard-core addicts who whiled away their spare hours in the basement watching wrestling videos. "It was not just a tabloid story. Newspapers thrive off this kind of thing," said Tim Baines, sports editor of the *Ottawa Sun*, who writes a weekly column on wrestling. "The murder-suicide peaks our interest because, in general, bad news is how we sell ourselves, that's how we sell newspapers. So we've got a murder-suicide, then you've got a famous wrestler. Then there's even more to it; maybe there's steroids involved. . . . This just blew up real fast." According to the Project for Excellence in Journalism's News Coverage Index, the case ranked eighth among network news TV stories for the week of June 24–29, with 4 percent of the newshole, the amount of airtime or print space available to report the news. For wrestling to register on the media scale was unprecedented in the PEJ's indices, especially since the news broke halfway through the week under study. On cable TV news, it ranked fifth with 7 percent and placed fourth in the PEJ's analysis of news talk shows at 7 percent. The following week, July 1–6, the aftermath of the murders remained prominent on cable news at 3 percent of the newshole, ranking sixth for the week. The emergence of YouTube as a source for archived news and commentary also kept the story rolling. More than five hundred video clips that focused on Benoit's death were posted on the Web site in the weeks following the incident.

The direction of the coverage — that was another matter. In recent years, the commentary media — the talking heads, the opinionated evening cable news shows, the print and online columnists — have become so pervasive that in some ways they have overwhelmed the work of the beat-the-streets, news-gathering media, replacing fact with rumor and speculation. "We don't live in a democracy; we live in a punditocracy," observed Douglas L. Battema, a communications professor at Western New England College who teaches sports journalism and has written about pro wrestling. "I think that's true of each and every part of our culture today. It's been taken over by commentary, which in many cases has replaced journalism and has replaced investigative reporting of any sort. Without question that has occurred, and it's affected the quality of the information people receive." As hard news relating to the Benoit case petered out after a few days, the story lived on, night after contentious night, on the talking-head circuit. "It was just a different field in terms of the attention it was going to get," said Alex Marvez of FOXSports.com, who covers wrestling for the Scripps Howard News Service. "Now you have all these competing news programs chasing the same subject in our Paris Hilton landscape, and wrestling made perfect sense. It is a compelling story anyway, let alone throwing in the wrestling."

The Raw Numbers

It didn't take long before nightly cable shows figured out that the Benoit case translated into ratings gold, especially for Nancy Grace, the sharp-tongued former prosecutor who hosts an hourlong justice-themed program on CNN Headline News. The first three nights of Benoit coverage in late June 2007 helped push her into thirteenth place in the key 25–54 demographic among weekday cable news and talk shows for June; she wasn't in the top twenty for that group in May. In her first sixteen shows following the tragedy, Grace led with Benoit eight times and used it in a supporting role three times. Her wrestling-themed shows attracted 46 percent more viewers than her non-wrestling shows. According to Nielsen Media Research, Grace averaged 148,000 viewers in the all-important (and core wrestling fan) age 25–54 category during May 2007. Every one of her eleven Benoit-related telecasts exceeded that average, with a whopping 355,000 watching June 28 for the appearance of Chris Jericho, one of Benoit's best friends.

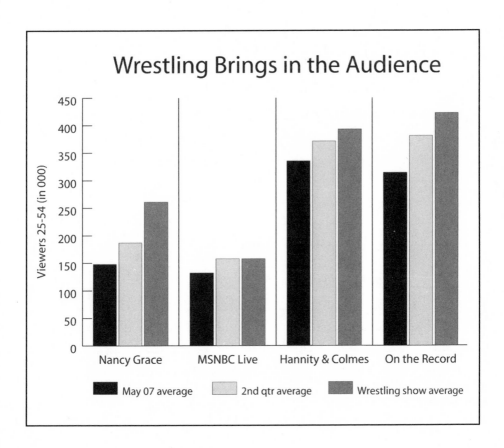

ROID RAGE EQUALS RATINGS

Viewers for cable news and talk shows, adults 25–54, in 000s
Wrestling-themed shows in bold

	Nancy Grace	MSNBC Live	Hannity & Colmes	On the Record
May average	148	132	335	314
June average	219	134	366	385
QTR 2 2007 average	187	158	371	381
Wrestling show average	261	158	393	422
6/26	**343**	**274**	442	458
6/27	**338**	**205**	385	**453**
6/28	**355**	**201**	599	608
6/29	**220**	no show	275	**340**
7/2	**266**	**103**	405	507
7/3	143	**183**	379	348
7/5	257	**141**	307	344
7/6	129	no show	**373**	302
7/9	**294**	**116**	436	322
7/10	245	**147**	**303**	382
7/11	**207**	**145**	487	403
7/12	154	**158**	375	394
7/13	**175**	no show	302	**300**
7/16	223	**148**	321	361
7/17	**184**	**70**	**374**	**389**
7/18	233	169	**404**	**356**

Excludes Fourth of July due to repeats and pre-emptions.
Source: Nielsen Media, MediaBistro.com, GeorgiaWrestlingHistory.com

Perhaps the most remarkable streak was pulled off by *MSNBC Live with Dan Abrams*, which allocated parts of twelve consecutive telecasts to the story. The show posted huge jumps over *Scarborough Country*, its predecessor in the time spot, which averaged 132,000 viewers in the 25–54 demographic for May. The first three nights of *MSNBC Live* of Benoit coverage all topped 200,000, with a high of 274,000 on June 26. Two of the three highest rated cable news shows, FOX News' *Hannity & Colmes* and *On the Record w/ Greta* (Van Susteren) also scored a windfall in the adult demographic coveted by advertisers. *Hannity & Colmes* attracted 599,000 viewers on June 28 — about 220,000 more than usual — for a show with "Superstar" Billy Graham and Debra Marshall, the ex-wife of Steve Austin. The talk tag team went with the Benoit flow for part of the airtime of six straight nights; six of the nine wrestling-oriented *Hannity & Colmes* shows scored above their average for both May and the second quarter. Van Susteren registered her two highest viewerships during the three-week period after the murders with shows that included ex-wrestlers Joanie "Chyna" Laurer and Ted DiBiase. Both wrestlers added at least 120,000 viewers to her average tally.

Members of the audience became more discriminating as the story dragged on, tuning out when they encountered stale information and observations. Larry King bombed in the July 9 ratings when he lobbed softballs at several wrestlers on his CNN program. (Among his genteel queries: "John, what did you make of this? How did you hear of it?" "Ted, what do you make of this?" "Steve, what's your read?") King scored 260,000 target viewers, 8.5 percent below his second quarter average and 34,000 fewer viewers than Grace logged just an hour earlier. MSNBC's viewership also subsided within a few days, perhaps because it too often relied on the same faces for analysis — Marc Mero appeared on ten of Abrams's twelve wrestling programs. After three weeks, fans were exhausted, and some of the lowest adult viewerships occurred July 17, following the release of a medical report that showed Benoit had massive levels of testosterone in his system. In all, though, ratings were normal or above average for twenty-seven of the thirty-eight episodes of the four talk shows that devoted the most extensive time to the story. The print media played a role in spreading the news too. Unlike the inconsequential Guerrero coverage, *The New York Times* dedicated eight stories and 4,448 words to Benoit. The *Los Angeles Times* spent almost 3,500 words on the subject, or almost ninety times as much as it generated on Guerrero.

THE FIRST WAVE: THE SEARCH FOR THE FACTS

The Benoit story passed through three waves of press coverage: the search for the facts, the search for an explanation, and the search for a larger meaning. The waves are not mutually exclusive; they raced one another, overlapped, and frequently capped and crested at the same time. But they offer a convenient way of tracking the evolution of the biggest wrestling story in the history of North America, from a murder investigation to a commentary on the state of professional sports.

From the outset, general news reporters found they were dealing with a difficult business to crack. Pro wrestling is mostly off-limits to outside scrutiny, as protective as a magician's guild, with its own circumspect, carnival-rooted lingo. "The world of wrestling is completely different, and it's hard to get a perspective on it if you haven't followed it very, very closely for a number of years," said Bryan Alvarez, editor of F4Wonline. com (*Figure Four Weekly* newsletter) and co-author of *The Death of WCW.* "If you mention something that's commonplace in wrestling to somebody who doesn't follow wrestling, they can't even begin to fathom how strange some of this stuff is."

A lot of outsiders were dumbfounded by wwe's first major decision — to air a three-hour tribute to Benoit on USA Network in place of its June 25 edition of the Monday night *Raw* even as news about the deaths reverberated around cyberspace. Many wrestling insiders, bloggers, and fans gave wwe a pass on the propriety of the show, citing the uncertain rush of information the company was sorting through as production time neared. More typical was the reaction of Doug Frattallone, a veteran TV reporter, producer and anchor, who pens the widely syndicated "Professor Wrestling" column: "If there's police tape around the home of one of your employees — and your employee and his family is inside, deceased — that might be a signal there's foul play. It's certainly not the time to immortalize someone. Either do a generic show, or have USA run a movie. What went on the air was maddening, especially since the rumor was out early in the day that it might have been a murder-suicide." The next day, WWE erased Benoit from its history books but the episode raised suspicions among reporters. "I can see how it is a dilemma. I don't know what I would do," said sports business expert Darren Rovell of CNBC. "But I do know that having run that, glorifying Benoit — who doesn't deserve any type of tribute — McMahon needed to come on again and say something to the effect that, in retrospect, deifying Chris Benoit was probably the wrong thing to do."

With a steep learning curve and skepticism about WWE's credibility, it's easy to see why reporters who stepped into wrestling for the first time exercised extra precaution to get the facts straight. John Hollis, who covered the story for the *Atlanta Journal-Constitution*, said the biggest challenge he faced was verifying information. "You call the WWE and they've obviously got their own agenda for whatever they're doing. You have to be really cautious with what information you do receive; not really cynical, but just keep in mind what you're dealing with," he said. "You're under competition to get stories, but then you mention the blogosphere, the Internet, and all this other stuff. For every one bit of truth that might be coming out of there, it seems like there are a hundred more leads you might follow that are nothing. So it makes you work a lot harder. You really want to stay up to date."

Nowhere was that task more evident than in a flap over an entry in Wikipedia, an open-source online encyclopedia, that appeared to foretell of Nancy Benoit's death fourteen hours before it occurred. With a whiff of conspiracy usually associated with Oliver Stone movies, the press and law enforcement officials tried to track down the source of the entry, which claimed Benoit missed a June 24 pay-per-view event because of Nancy's death. Complicating matters, an unidentified poster made the entry using an Internet protocol address registered in Stamford, Connecticut, the home base of WWE. Were the Benoit murders premeditated? Was WWE involved? Was Benoit 'fessing up on Wikipedia using a corporate computer? The breathless media search for answers actually crossed the international dateline. In Australia, the *Sydney Morning Herald* reported that a computer linked to the case belonged to a Sydney resident. Back home, using Internet clues, CNETNews.com singled out a University of Connecticut student by name and, rather irrelevant to the topic at hand, revealed the suspect's MySpace page, which said he wanted to sleep with his friend's sister. The Wikipedia angle ended up as a red herring — the anonymous poster stepped forward on June 28, saying he had posted a wild-eyed rumor and nothing more, though one of Grace's guests, former FBI investigator Mike Brooks, still asked five days later about what the poster knew and when he knew it.

The lack of familiarity with wrestling's ground rules showed in other ways too. In a knowing fashion, Grace said on June 27 that Benoit might have been unhinged because he was demoted from the Four Horsemen group to *Raw*. Benoit hadn't been a part of that wrestling clique since 1999 and that was back in a now-defunct rival promotion. The next night, *The O'Reilly Factor* left fans aghast when the flamboyant Geraldo Rivera hinted

Benoit as part of The Four Horsemen in wcw.

that Kevin Sullivan, Nancy Benoit's ex-husband and a former wrestler, might have been involved in the Benoit deaths and the death of wrestler Sherri (Russell) Martel, who died June 15.

> *Rivera*: The authorities say that here is Chris Benoit. He kills his wife, Nancy, on Friday, June 15, or Saturday, June 16 [sic]. Do you know that on Friday, June 15, a woman named Sherri Martel also died of unnatural causes related to drug use. Who is Sherri Martel? She is another woman connected to this group of professional wrestlers. Indeed, the guy who was the original husband of Chris's wife, Nancy, the one he allegedly murdered, he was this other woman['s], this Sherri Martel's booker and friend. And she died the same day, Bill — June 15, Friday, June 15.

> *Bill O'Reilly*: So they were all in the same industry, the wrestling industry.

> *Rivera*: Same industry. They all knew each other, they were all connected. It's one degree of separation.

Then later:

> *Rivera*: I think this is going to be gigantic. This will affect WWE. We don't know if it's a double murder-suicide or something more insidious. Maybe it's a triple murder. Maybe it's a quadruple murder.

Despite those missteps, the role of the news-gathering media, both print and online, was valuable in the search for facts. In addition to reporting the straight news from Georgia authorities — that the case was a double murder-suicide with some bizarre twists — old-fashioned record checks and detective work produced important stories. Within hours, S. A. Reid and Kathy Jefcoats reported in the *Atlanta Journal-Constitution* that Nancy Benoit had filed for divorce in 2003 and sought a protective order against her husband for alleged domestic violence. The TMZ.com Web site posted the divorce papers the next day. In Albany, New York, far from the murder site, the *Times Union* linked Benoit to a local steroid investigation in a June 26 exclusive. Reporter Brendan J. Lyons revealed Benoit was a regular customer of a Florida clinic whose operators had pleaded guilty to prescription drug charges in Albany County. The *Boston Herald* advanced the story by tracking down Holly McFague, a Benoit neighbor who guided police to the premises and corrected some timeline issues. To underscore the immediacy that the Internet can bring to journalism, Dan Chernau accurately reported the details of the deaths on WrestlingClassics.com on June 26, including the style of chokehold Benoit used to kill his son, based on his conversation with a reporter. As Chernau noted, authorities confidentially briefed reporters about their findings, so the Internet became a release point for authenticated reports that otherwise didn't make it into print for days. The *Atlanta Journal-Constitution* also provided detailed information about Dr. Philip Astin's medical background after authorities conducted raids on his office, stemming from pre-scriptions he wrote for Benoit. Within a few days, though, much of the hard news started to dry up, and discussion of the Benoit story turned to a second and all-consuming wave.

The media was "on the juice."

~

THE SECOND WAVE:
THE SEARCH FOR AN EXPLANATION

What went on inside the mind of the killer? What was he think-ing? "I don't think we'll ever be able to wrap our minds around it completely," Fayette County district attorney Scott Ballard said at his first press conference. A lot of the commentary media would beg to differ. Sam Ford, project manager at the Con-vergence Culture Consortium for Massachusetts Institute of Technology's (MIT) program in Comparative Media Studies, pointed out that the function of the media isn't always clear, especially in a case such as Benoit's. "Do we seek for the news to report? Or are we asking it to provide closure and provide answers?" asked Ford, who has co-taught a wrestling course at MIT and worked as a wrestling manager. "It seems like, at least in this case, a lot of the news coverage, even while seeming very objective, was seeking to provide an answer. It's always easier to say, 'An unspeakable tragedy happened tonight and it was because of A.' You can never really provide closure because no one will ever know what happened. But it sounded like a neat little bundle the media could put it in, and, from a commercial standpoint, creating an easy answer seems more marketable."

One possible explanation for the tragedy appeared to lie in Delta, British Columbia — an unlikely breeding ground for a media feeding frenzy. On June 26, Vancouver radio station CKWX reported that Pam Winthrope, a Delta woman, believed Daniel Benoit suffered from Fragile X syndrome, an inherited developmental impairment, based on a conversation her late husband had with Benoit five years earlier. Her recollection became a flashpoint for anyone trying to get inside Benoit's psyche. At breakneck speed, all elements of the press — with a helping hand from WWE — sped down one of the most reckless and slipshod paths this side of *Weekly World News*. The top WWE brass quickly asserted that Fragile X was at the heart of the discord between Benoit and his wife. "I think it's fair to say that the subject of caring for that child was part of what made their relationship complicated and difficult, and it's something they were both constantly struggling with," WWE lawyer Jerry McDevitt told the Associated Press. "We do know it was a source of stress and consternation." For its part, much of the media dropped any pretense of nuance. Daniel was described as "mentally retarded," "physically stunted," "mentally disabled," and "autistic-like." The New York *Daily News*, seldom troubled by conventions of good taste, screamed, "The Tragic Family Secret Benoit Hid from World," in its June 28 edition. WWE CEO Linda McMahon added to the furor when she appeared on *Good Morning America* June 28. As an image of the *Daily News* story and a crawl asking, "Was It a Battle over Disabled Son?" filled the screen, McMahon said:

As we found out literally over the last forty-eight hours, we found out about Daniel's illness, which we did not know. . . . That's what the focus of this is really turning more to, the tension of what must have been happening between a husband and a wife over the management, and the schooling, and the rearing of this child with mental retardation.

It is alarming that so many accounts sprung from the flimsiest of evidence — a five-year-old phone call related secondhand by a Canadian housewife. It was accepted as a given. There was no physical evidence in the postmortem to determine if Daniel had Fragile X, but a higher standard of diligence was in order. The day after McMahon appeared on *Good Morning America*, Daniel's maternal grandparents, through their lawyer, challenged the assertion that the child had Fragile X syndrome. In short order, prosecutor Ballard said July 3 that a check of Daniel's medical records and an interview with his kindergarten teacher contradicted the claims. Armed with that new information, WWE reversed course, as spokesman Gary Davis said, "We were just as caught up as everyone else. . . . I think we have to go with what the district attorney has said as being the best up-to-date information available right now."

But once a misleading story enters cyberspace, it's there forever. On July 15, long after doubts were cast, Alfonso A. Castillo reported in *Newsday*, "Benoit's work schedule left him little time to spend with Daniel, 7, who reportedly suffered from Fragile X — a form of mental retardation often mistaken for autism." Marvez offered a sharp critique of the incident: "It was horrendous and perpetuated by WWE, as well. To go ahead and report that on the air; yes, it made sense on some levels — maybe the kid had something wrong. But to say something without proof and then to have WWE perpetuate it and say that their understanding was that the kid had Fragile X looked like their way to try to put an explanation to what Chris Benoit did. It was as bad journalistically as you can get, taking something that's reported from a phone call from someone whose husband is dead and going with it as fact."

Although the stories about Fragile X waned, conjecture about the role steroids played in the murders intensified. For nearly four weeks, steroids were front and center in much of the coverage, whether it concerned Benoit's abundant personal use, loopholes in the WWE wellness policy, or the startling announcement that Dr. Astin dispensed ten months' worth of steroids to the wrestler every few weeks. In a strange way, the timing of the murders was fortuitous; they occurred when Barry Bonds was chasing baseball's all-time home run record with allegations of steroids swirling about him. As Kevin Eck, who blogs about wrestling for the *Baltimore Sun*, noted, the genie was out of the bottle and wouldn't soon return under his own power. "I remember watching the news conference they held in Atlanta, and as soon as the question was asked, 'Were steroids found in the house?' and they answered affirmatively, I knew right then and there that the media was just going to jump on it and run with it because steroids are such a hot-button topic," he said.

Eck's instincts were correct. Less than three hours after Ballard announced June 26 that law enforcement officials would analyze the drugs they found in Benoit's house, WWE issued an aggressive reprimand to reporters and pundits, noting Benoit's prescriptions were perfectly legal. "Steroids were not, and could not, be related to the cause of death," the federation said, later adding, "WWE strongly suggests that it is entirely wrong for speculators to suggest that steroids had anything to do with these senseless acts." Better, in retrospect, to have wished King Canute good luck in holding back the tide. The headlines alone told the story:

"Murder-Suicide Looks Like 'Roid Rage, Expert Says"
— *Vancouver Sun*

"Wrestler May Have Had 'Roid Rage"
— *Herald-Leader* (Lexington, Kentucky)

"Wrestle Maniac's 'Roid Rage: Inside a Killer's Doomed Love Tale"
— *New York Post*

"Steroid Rage at Work? Inside the Wrestler Murder Mystery"
— ABCNews.com

References to "roid rage" were universal across all forms of the media. A LexisNexis database search revealed 287 newspaper stories that referenced the term "roid rage" in the context of the Benoit story. Another 147 "roid rage" references came in Benoit-related pieces on newswires and press releases. In all, the LexisNexis search returned 532 media hits for the terms *Benoit* and *roid rage*.

To investigate the steroid issue made perfect sense, although the method of the killings — done over a weekend, with Bibles placed near Nancy and Daniel — suggested they were anything but the product of a drug-induced fit. Even medical experts agreed that the subject was worth exploring; the Associated Press quoted the first reaction of Linn Goldberg, head of the division of health promotion and sports medicine at Oregon Health Sciences University, upon hearing of the murders: "Check for steroids." But the day-in, day-out suppositions shed little light on the subject, and even played in the back of the minds of print reporters. "This mad rush to beat the Internet, to beat the talking heads on TV, journalists need to be careful not to let the mad rush to get the story stop [them] from doing what's right," said Hollis of the Atlanta paper. "You've got TV on it, or *Nancy Grace*, or something like that, and you don't want to feel like you're missing something." As one example, Abrams, the MSNBC host, persisted in steroid-related questioning through the saga. "I know the WWE doesn't want us to use the word *steroid*. I know — and I'm not saying we know it was steroids because we don't. But it is a totally legitimate question to ask, isn't it?" he inquired during the June 28 program. Five days later, he noted, "In the murder-suicide investigation of former WWE wrestler Chris Benoit, the debate rages. Did steroids, could steroids have played a role in his murder of his wife and son?" On July 16, Abrams devoted a portion of his show to what Benoit's toxicology report, scheduled for release the next day, might say about steroids. For input, he turned to former FBI profiler Cliff Van Zandt, who pulled double duty; he also was on earlier in the show commenting about a National Guard sniper shooting in Wyoming. The emphasis on steroids prompted some of the sharpest rejoinders from current and past wrestlers, who dismissed the theory out of hand. On *Larry King Live*, WWE champ John Cena explained, "I take great offense to not only people of the media pointing to this as being a case of 'roid rage when there hasn't been any proof of that, but also pointing a finger at WWE as a whole, saying that we're all just a bunch of steroid monsters." At the funeral of Daniel and Nancy Benoit, WWE announcer Jim Ross made headlines when he declared, "This is not about steroids. That horse needs to be put in the barn." But the "roid rage" explanation was convenient and sufficiently plausible for the press to continue with it. On July 11, Grace hosted Penny Bordeau-Durham, the wife of the late Johnny Grunge, who talked about her husband's battles with "roid rages." "One time, we were — you know, we were just having a conversation and talking, and you know, just — and drank a couple beers, and he just went off, and he came after me with the butcher knife. And I got down on my knees and I just started praying — and I just started praying, and then it just started dissipating." In the view of British journalist John

Lister, author of *Turning the Tables: The Story of Extreme Championship Wrestling*, personal accounts such as Bordeau-Durham's resonated with viewers and kept the focus on steroids. "Many people will have personal experience of the other contributing factors, such as depression, marital disputes, problems with the son, and so on, but have not committed murder themselves, so it feels less plausible as a cause. Because so few people have any experience of heavy steroid use, it's easier to 'believe' it was the major factor, whether or not that is the case in reality."

The Third Wave:
The Search for a Larger Meaning

When pro wrestling lands on the editorial pages of prominent newspapers, it's a sure sign that it's crossed the radar of media opinion leaders. Editorial writers and prominent sportswriters set off a third wave of coverage when they seized on the Benoit murders to opine about the state of professional sports in general and pro wrestling in particular. "After a while, a story takes on such a life of its own," said David Skolnick, co-publisher and co-editor of *Wrestling Perspective*, who also covers politics and city hall for *The Vindicator* in Youngstown, Ohio. "We have tabloid TV and tabloid publications taking care of this story first. Then the mainstream media says, 'Well, that's interesting; maybe we'll do a story on it.' The columnists and the top fifty newspapers were getting involved in formulating opinions, but it wasn't immediate. It was again that same attitude of, 'It's more suited for supermarket tabloids than for me.'" With that touch of condescension, newspapers across the country agreed wrestling's buffoonery had morphed into dangerous buffoonery:

Augusta Chronicle, July 9: Drug abuse in pro wrestling may not have been taken seriously to this point because hardly anyone takes pro wrestling seriously. Except that there are lots of devoted fans, many of them young and impressionable — and now three more people are dead.

Dallas Morning News, July 7: We hope the death of wrestling hero Chris Benoit, who brutally killed his wife and his son before taking his own life, will be a watershed moment in which wrestling confronts its nasty underbelly — and cleans it up. Professional wrestling must end its cash-register-ringing and shadowy wink-wink association with painkillers and steroids.

Times Union (Albany, New York), July 28: Professional wrestling — really, where's the prefix "un" when you need it — used to be a harmless enough mix of faux sport and more genuine freak show. . . . Only now there's this problem in a world where regulation is little more than a rumor. Steroids are present in wrestling, too, just like in other sports with real rules and some means of enforcing them.

Benoit is stretched by the late Louie Spicolli.

For better or worse, it might have taken a sensational double murder-suicide to get the press to sit up and take notice. "The only reason this story got the play it did was because a mother and child also died. If it were just Benoit killing himself, the story would have gotten one one-thousandth of the play it did, which is really, really sad," said Frattallone, who monitors and places video clips for TV station Web sites. "Wrestlers dying way too young has been a huge story for years, but the mainstream media simply won't make time for it unless a particular story has a tragic twist, as Benoit's did." Few outcries were heard after the deaths of Louie Spicolli, Brian Pillman, Davey Boy Smith, Curt Hennig, Rick Rude, Eddie Guerrero, or any pro wrestlers who died at an early age because of steroid-, drug-, or health-related issues. A sobering 2004 study by *USA Today* found at least sixty-five wrestlers of age forty-five or younger have died since 1997, twenty-five from heart attacks or other coronary problems. Five deaths were attributed in part to steroids; twelve others cited evidence of painkillers, cocaine, and other drugs. For *The Sun* (UK), Lister and Simon Rothstein compiled a list of forty-one full-time pros, up from eighteen during the previous decade, who died between 1997 and 2007. Those numbers were twisted like pretzels during coverage of the Benoit story — several NBC correspondents relied on a count of sixty wrestlers under the age of sixty-five who had died since 1985, while wrestling's defenders picked apart each list, eliminating deaths that had no connection to drugs. "The list can be argued either way," Lister noted. "Very few of the deaths can be conclusively proven to be wrestling's 'fault,' but equally there are very few where you can conclusively say wrestling was not a contributing factor." The exact count is less important than the trend, of course, and wrestling's "Book of the Dead" produced some meaningful mainstream commentary about the state of the business. Jason Whitlock of the *Kansas City Star* reminded readers that because wrestlers have no union and no health benefits, they're often used and then discarded by the business:

> No one weeps for the wrestler who dies way too young or lives as a cripple, addicted to painkillers by age 45. No one cares about their exploitation. It's like the men who entertained many of us during our childhood are some-how magically categorized as nonhuman because they participate in a "sports event" with a predetermined out-come. . . . Those of us in the media should care enough to complain loudly. We're the watchdogs. We're the voice of the voiceless. We don't have to respect the "sport" to appreciate the humanity of the performers.

Writing in the *Palm Beach Post*, Hal Habib carefully cata-logued some of the major deaths and explored the sad statistic that wrestlers are dying at seven times the national average. "Pro-fessional wrestlers don't hurt each other. They hurt themselves. They do it with recreational drugs, performance-enhancing drugs, risky in-ring maneuvers, painkillers to mask the effects of those maneuvers, and sometimes a lethal cocktail of all of the above." Unfortunately, a reasoned search for meaning and context in the Benoit case was bogged down amid a spree of finger-pointing, a determination to identify heroes and villains, and a quest for entertaining television. How else to explain the presence of Mark Fuhrman — yes, the rogue detective in the O.J. Simpson case — on *Hannity & Colmes*, suggesting that some other sinister force was at work. "So far, I would be very suspicious that we don't have another party involved in this crime. I'm not sure Chris Benoit even committed suicide," he said more than a week after Georgia officials labeled the event a double murder-suicide. McMahon became a lightning rod for critics such as Jim Litke of the Associated Press, who maintained the WWE honcho would still have been in hiding over his fake assassination on Monday night *Raw* if not for Benoit. "If there's a hysteria around his 'sport,' all he has to do is pause in front of a mirror to find the huckster who's responsible," Litke said. WWE wrestlers leaped to the defense of their boss, including an online missive from Ken Kennedy: "Saying that Vince McMahon is responsible for the deaths of the Benoits is like saying that you and I are responsible for the deaths of Anna Nicole Smith and her son. . . . Somebody, PLEASE, stop the insanity!!!!" On cable TV, names touted as primetime experts about the state of wrestling sounded like a mid-1980s fanfest lineup: The Ultimate Warrior, Jacques Rougeau, Billy Graham, and Lanny Poffo. Steve Blackman and Marc Mero engaged in a poor man's version of the Lincoln-Douglas debate on several shows, including *MSNBC Live*:

Blackman: Marc, I mean, we're not familiar with the drug taking in there like when we were in there ourselves to witness it.

Mero: It's still happening.

By turning the search for perspective and context into a shouting match, the cable news shows demonstrated that they're not all that different from the sport they were covering. "They're looking for Mero and Blackman. They want to go back and forth over personal responsibility or whether Vince is evil," said Larry DeGaris, a professor and director of sports marketing programs at the University of Indianapolis, also known as wrestler Larry Brisco. "That's just the structure of their shows. It's a joke, but it's good theater." Then DeGaris turned to wrestling jargon to sum up the nightly gabfests. "You've got your babyface and your heel. It was all phony. It was all a work."

ENDGAME:
OPPORTUNITIES GAINED AND LOST

The active pursuit of the story ended July 17 when investigators released a toxicology report that showed that Benoit had elevated levels of testosterone in his system, and probably took testosterone cypionate within hours of his death. His 220-pound frame was pumped full of synthetic testosterone; a test that compares hormones found his testosterone-to-epitestosterone ratio was 59:1; for athletes, 4:1 is considered acceptable and

1:1 is considered normal, while WWE permitted 10:1 with some caveats. Georgia medical examiner Dr. Kris Sperry downplayed the role of steroids in the death, and WWE took that report as a bill of health for its wellness policy. McDevitt and David Black, president of a laboratory in Nashville, Tennessee, that runs the WWE testing program, made the rounds explaining Benoit tested positive for testosterone and negative for anabolic steroids. Sperry clearly said he found "no illegal anabolic steroids" in Benoit, McDevitt told Pat Lalama, who subbed for Grace on July 17. "The drug-testing program, we believe, has been very effective in working. And it worked with respect to Chris Benoit." One of the conditions WWE exacted from the show was that McDevitt and Black would speak uninterrupted by industry reporters Meltzer and Alvarez. When Lalama turned to those two, they were ready with rebuttals. Alvarez stressed the U.S. Drug Enforcement Agency considers testosterone and anabolic steroids to be the same thing. "So the question is, 'Why are WWE wrestlers, no matter what the levels are, allowed to be taking anabolic steroids? Especially in Chris Benoit's case with a level of 59:1 ratio.'" Others were just as skeptical. In New York, *Daily News* sportswriter Christian Red declared WWE to be "in full spin control" and quoted Dr. Gary Wadler, a member of the World Anti-Doping Agency, dismissing WWE's argument that synthetic testosterone did not amount to an anabolic steroid. For the press, though, that was it. "They reached a conclusion. There's nothing to wait for, there's no suspense," DeGaris said. "I am surprised at how fast it died. The tox test comes back; it's the WWE's worst fear, and nothing happened. But in the end, it gets back to the media's view of wrestling. It's like, 'We know pro wrestlers are a bunch of 'roided-up freaks. This should come as a surprise?'" In part, the way the media closed the book on Benoit might reflect how both it and the culture have evolved in the early days of the twenty-first century — Chris Benoit tonight, Lindsay Lohan tomorrow, and an astronaut wearing diapers the day after that. "When something like this happens again, and it will, there'll be another flurry of coverage and [then] we'll go back to business as usual," said Battema of Western New England College. "One of the ways that our culture has developed around TV and the Internet is that nothing has any kind of staying power. Everything is temporary, fleeting, and insubstantial in a lot of ways."

After nearly four weeks of coverage in every possible medium, the press botched more spots than a pair of teenage preliminary wrestlers at the local armory. Republican congressman Cliff Stearns of Florida, author of two bills to set steroid testing standards in pro sports, released a statement July 6 that called for a congressional investigation. He received virtually no attention until reporters started calling him July 9. "Amazing," mused Chernau of WrestlingClassics.com. "Every lunatic theory gets picked up in two seconds flat and actual news takes three days."

On *Good Morning America*, host Robin Roberts failed to follow up with Linda McMahon on the source of her Fragile X information. Meredith Viera was slightly harsher with Vince

McMahon when he defended the company's wellness policy on *The Today Show*. But she never pushed him to answer whether wrestlers should be allowed to take steroids under prescription, one of several loopholes in the wellness program that the dealings with Astin appeared to exploit. When an indictment filed against Astin charged that he wrote illegal prescriptions to wrestlers with the initials of OG and MJ, it took most of the press a day to figure out what wrestling fans instinctively knew — Oscar Gutiérrez (Rey Mysterio) and Mark Jindrak. "If you turn on TV and see how little Rey Mysterio is, and find out he has a link to steroids, then you have every reason to believe every person in professional wrestling, is taking steroids," Skolnick said. "As a fan and a journalist, I was saying, 'You need to understand the drug policy. You're not asking the right questions.'"

But the Benoit case provided opportunities for a few parts of the press to shine. While the commentary media's contribution was a mixed bag, at best, a lot of print outlets clearly enlightened casual readers. The best coverage came from the trade publications, and Meltzer, so close to the business, dug into the fine print and explained the nitty-gritty in a way that the mainstream media could not. An odd symbiosis developed between the trade press and *Nancy Grace*, in particular. Grace's producers started turning to Marvez and Alvarez to learn more about guests under consideration — who was angling for a WWE gig, who was credible within the industry, who was not. "She was clueless on day one," said Meltzer, "but by the end, she kind of got it. It became the go-to show because at least she had guests like Konnan [Charles Ashenoff] who had something to say. She ended up understanding the ramifications better than some of the WWE wrestlers." That is a valuable lesson for journalists on any story of this magnitude — learn from people who know more than you do. The Benoit story also showed how the Internet plays an increasing role in spreading news. The message board at WrestlingClassics. com, one of the most popular wrestling Web sites, filled to the breaking point with news, gossip, and posts. It became a clearinghouse for YouTube clips and quick newspaper reads, and moderators had to close down one thread after it reached a hundred pages. "It was fascinating to see how people who follow wrestling wanted more information, so they went to the online coverage and the discussion threads," said Ford of MIT. "In real time, a more complete story was probably available on that site for people who knew a little about wrestling than you would have found in any of the other coverage because it included all the bits and pieces."

Laugh at it or cry about it, media coverage of the Benoit case made important people pay attention. Two congressional committees announced plans to look into wrestling's body count and WWE's drug-testing policies. In both cases, lawmakers cited the work of reporters as justification for their probes. "Investigations by journalists have described a culture of performance-enhancing drug use in professional wrestling, high fatality rates among young professional wrestlers, and an inability or unwillingness of WWE to address these problems," wrote Reps. Henry Waxman, D-California, and Tom Davis, R-Virginia, chairman and ranking member respectively, of the House Oversight and Government Reform Committee. In that sense, the press performed one of its duties, however unintentional. It set the stage for a public debate on a topic that clearly alarmed citizens who, just a few weeks before, had no more than a passing knowledge of pro wrestling. Seven weeks after Benoit took three lives, the wife of former WWE and WCW wrestler Brian "Crush" Adams found her husband unconscious at their Tampa, Florida, home; he was dead at forty-three. In other times, the mainstream press would have noted his passing with little more than a brief obituary. But the Benoit story so energized the press that rules of the game had changed. More than three hundred stories on Adams appeared in the first twenty-four hours after he died. An Associated Press story alluded to the steroids found in Benoit's house, though toxicology and tissue sample results were weeks away. On *Nancy Grace*, a guest host turned to Meltzer and Mero for expert opinions, and Adams became the lead story on the Yahoo.com sports page, ahead of the death of Hall of Fame baseball star Phil Rizzuto. Several reporters, energized by investigations into drug use in sports, shredded what little credibility the WWE wellness policy had by linking name after name to illegal steroid pipelines. About a dozen stars, including Randy Orton and Ken Kennedy — who maintained publicly that the wellness program forced him off the juice — were still receiving steroid bundles in early 2007,

A flying crossbody on Honky Tonk Wayne in Calgary.

according to *Sports Illustrated*. "I don't think it's a bad thing for the spotlight to be out there," Kevin Eck said. "I know WWE gets ultra-defensive on these things, and you can't blame them for a lot of things that didn't happen on their watch. But they are the industry standard. When a wrestler dies now, it's going to make the tabloid shows. The flying under the radar is over."

DAY OF THE DEAD

PHOTO: MIKE LANO

DAY OF THE DEAD
Irvin Muchnick

Expired ... Defunct ... Departed ... Deceased ... Gone ... Perished ... Rubbed out ... Croaked ... Liquidated ... Sleeping with the fishes ... Rigor mortis ... Muerto ... Mort ... Deddo ... Blank-as-a-doornail ... Blank-right ...

A gruesome summer weekend at a gated mansion in the Atlanta exurbs confronted wrestling people with a question no amount of industrial-strength propaganda by the flacks of World Wrestling Entertainment, Inc. will ever be able to deflect.

The question is: Which part of "dead" don't you understand?

One of many sobering facets of the Chris Benoit story is the observation that wrestlers, those peerless practitioners of in-your-face entertainment, seem to get more squeamish than most when the conversation turns to the subject of mortality. Maybe it's just their realization of the brevity of their careers, which for many is indistinguishable from the fragility of their very identities.

"Ten wrestlers, twenty personalities. . . ." In short order we'll have more to say about how even Chris Benoit, in the end, may have been just another one of those guys who couldn't separate wrestling from life. First, let's just note that the wrestling community, for whatever reason, disproportionately deploys the lexicon of mobsters. Theirs is a form of expression simultaneously loaded with bluster and soaked to the gills in sentimentality. And both traits mask an essential cynicism.

Euphemistically, fallen colleagues are referred to as having "passed away." It's as though their last breaths were routinely gasped in hospice care at assisted-living facilities rather than in pools of vomit from drug overdoses. Systematically, and somewhat poignantly, wrestlers, promoters, and their great enablers, see-no-evil fans, keep their heads on an amoral swivel, avoiding the implications of this piece of unpleasant evidence or that bourgeois interpretation of right and wrong. Never has the psychological insecurity of folks whose stock-in-trade is physical courage, even physical intimidation, been on starker display.

That contemporary wrestling has a cult of death is not news. But with the Benoit scandal, the dimensions expand qualitatively. For the first time in modern memory, a troubled wrestler took out other people along with him, loved ones at that, thereby challenging the familiar paradigm of "mere" self-destruction.*

For the first time, because Benoit's acts were so heinous in the details, mainstream media climbed closer to the foothills of an adult attention span. Of course they didn't do so in ways satisfying to most readers of this book. Then again, when it comes to distorting facts in service of a juicy narrative, wrestling itself doesn't exactly represent the fullest flowering of the legacy of Edward R. Murrow — which gives that particular complaint a whiff of pettiness and hypocrisy. The eBay bidding floor quintuples for used DVD copies of *Hard Knocks: The Chris Benoit Story*, yet Nancy Grace can't pepper her reports of this *prima facie* sensational story with speculation and the random technical error? Give me a break.

Also for the first time, government agencies awoke from their usual deep slumber when it comes to examining one of the signature pop-culture phenomena of our times. In the past, wrestling hasn't just gotten a pass (or at least a sneer tantamount to a pass) from aficionados of "respectable" sports; it also has gotten a pat on the head from much of the crowd that targets rap lyrics as the last great fissure of western civilization. Because culture-bashing jihads have ideological symmetry — the left

---

* An article on SLAM! Wresling by British journalist Brian Elliott noted the 1944 murder-suicide of Charles "Gorilla Grubmeyer" Eastman and his wife. Jimmy "Superfly" Snuka was not charged in the 1983 death of his girlfriend, Nancy Argentino, but I am among those who believe the incident merited, at a minimum, his indictment for manslaughter.

hates the violence, the right hates the sex — wrestling heretofore has lucked out with its admixture of viscera and juvenalia. The people who most hate it are also the people most inclined to simply dismiss it.

Whether the flurry on Capitol Hill signaled anything more than a short-term interlude of invasiveness and inconvenience remained to be seen. But even if that development doesn't lead to wholesale reversal of the deregulatory regime of the 1980s, it's something. Along the same lines, a member of the World Wrestling Entertainment board of directors, Bob Bowman (also chief executive of Major League Baseball Advanced Media), mused aloud in *The New York Times* about the inadequacy of WWE drug testing. This is significant because the *Times* is the discussion board of the ruling class and WWE is a publicly traded company on the New York Stock Exchange.

We're still waiting to hear from the precinct of McMahon family pal Lowell Weicker Jr., another WWE board member and a former Connecticut senator and governor who always could be counted on to appoint Vince to a position within the Special Olympics when his image needed a fresh buff. Vince hasn't needed one this bad since he was indicted for conspiracy to distribute steroids in 1993. (The next year he was acquitted in federal court; five years after that, while playing lead heel in his TV troupe at the same time he was preparing an initial public stock offering, he falsely bragged that he'd been convicted of one count.)

While we navigate these heady corridors of power, let's extend further kudos to that fine institution in Fairfield, Sacred

Heart University, which chose Vince to deliver the 2007 commencement keynote. Sacred Heart trustee Linda McMahon, as stated on the university's Web site, is part of a "'power couple' [that] has taken America by storm. They have transformed the way we are entertained and, more subtly, provided powerful and generous assistance to Americans young and old." Young and old, but mostly young.

There's a last way Benoit altered the wrestling death cult: he officially made it recursive, something that turns in on itself, like a backfiring match stipulation. We're told that in his last year Chris Benoit fell into deep pits of depression, anxiety, and paranoia, leading to the grisly sequence that obliterated his family. His state of despair was catalyzed by watching others who were similarly depressed, stressed out, and used up — notably close friends Eddie Guerrero and Johnny Grunge — similarly implode, albeit in less dramatic fashion.

Then, in the wake of Benoit's suicide, you had the morbid spectacle of the wrestler as superfan, always a reliable tinderbox of displaced fantasies. There was a journeyman on the independent circuit named James Fawcett, who billed himself as "Devil Bhudakhan." Fawcett idolized Benoit, much as Benoit himself idolized the now retired and wheelchair-bound Tom "Dynamite Kid" Billington. Fawcett, like Benoit, also had marital problems. On July 15 — twenty days after the bodies of Chris, Nancy, and Daniel were found — Fawcett hung himself in his home near Pittsburgh. Was this wrestling's first copycat suicide?

(You may be wondering about Chris Von Erich, who in 1991 emulated his older brother Mike's death, four years earlier, by his own hand, and Kerry Von Erich, who in 1993 proactively followed younger brothers Mike and Chris, and older brother David [1984, non-suicidal sleeping pill reaction], into the beyond. But in my accounting the Von Erichs don't qualify as classic copycats, for their clan wrote its own inimitable playbook of dysfunction and pathology. Besides, each offed himself with a different method: Mike deliberately ODing on Placidyl [ethchlorvynol], the same drug that killed David; Chris shooting himself in the head; and Kerry turning a gun on his chest.)

Success as a wrestler requires both the mental toughness to navigate backstage politics and the physical toughness to take bumps under the klieg lights for the edification of us naïve ticket buyers. It's unsettling to ponder how an athlete with those attributes could, when the cheering stops, be as divorced from reality as the "mark" in the third row, but there you have it.

Lance Evers (former wrestler Lance Storm) — easily the smartest insider voice in post-Benoit commentary — noted that while "kayfabe" is dead, in the sense that everyone acknowledges wrestling's "worked" or staged nature, vestiges of the old carnival code of cagey swerving linger in ways that hamstring common sense. "Everyone still spins and denies out of habit," Evers said. "Steroids and pain pills are a real problem, yet no one wants to admit what is painfully obvious. Now is the time for cleaning up this business and saving lives."

McMahon can't grasp this, I think, because he badly needs to control. The need is so freakish it can trump self-interest. You can see the dynamic in the debate over lighter travel and predictable vacation schedules for the talent. *The Pro Wrestling Torch's* Wade Keller pointed out that, in an era built around pay-per-views, with far fewer house shows, there are sane solutions to this problem. But WWE resists them, probably because management calculates that a little mental autonomy could grow into a very bad thing. You can't have the inmates running the asylum or the animals calling the shots at the circus.

Evers, who now operates a training school, also was astute in assessing the evolution of the lifestyle. "For me, wrestling was a career, nothing more, nothing less," he said. Though passion is fine, dreams of a certain zealotry expose fundamental misconceptions of what should be the wrestler's first rule: self-preservation. For my money, some of the most dangerous trends of today's wrestling scene had nothing to do with steroids. They were initiated by the can-you-top-this? stunt artists of the old ECW and by Mick Foley, one of the all-time sloppy bodies, who made a fetish (as well as the bestseller lists) out of his capacity to absorb ill-advised bumps, disfigurement, and non-gimmicked pain. Benoit, like The Dynamite Kid, regularly did diving head butts off the top rope, even after missing a year of action with a broken neck. He also took chair shots to the back of the head, "which is stupid," anti-concussion crusader and former wrestler Chris Nowinski said.

PHOTO: MIKE LANO

A diving head butt from Benoit's Pegasus Kid.

The point of professional wrestling is not to get hurt; it is to look like you're getting hurt while not doing so. The end of kayfabe has presented us with a postmodern conundrum, a generation of numbskulls who are nothing more than marks for themselves.

By now you must understand that if you turned to this essay expecting a tearjerker, you should redirect your energies toward tracking down the third violinist at your local symphony. If you're interested in the science of testosterone-to-epitestosterone ratios, you should seek out your friendly neighborhood gym rat. The instant topic is death in wrestling, as an idea. A lot of deaths, against the backdrop of a common workplace, a cluster that surely would set off alarms at the Centers for Disease

Control and Prevention or the Occupational Safety and Health Administration if the victims weren't cartoon characters too few people regard as actual human beings. Deaths, of a volume statistically and actuarially impossible outside the discipline of epidemiology and the dimmest concept of public health.

Discussion of a death syndrome requires a death list, and these days everyone has one. At the most understated end of the spectrum, there are WWE's own preemptive bullet points, a grand total of five guys who kicked the bucket on the company's watch: Brian Pillman (1997, heart attack); Owen Hart (1999, stunt fall); Thomas Russell Haas (2001, heart attack); Eddie Guerrero (2005, heart attack caused by "old" alcohol and drug abuse); Chris Benoit (2007, "monster"). (Left unclear is whether this short list is intended to go all the way back to Vince's grandfather Jess McMahon, who in house history invented pro wrestling before Vincent James McMahon reinvented it and Vincent Kennedy McMahon came along to re-reinvent it.)

McMahon's minions have a rather crabbed definition of "on the company's watch": they mean that the deceased was under contract at the precise second when the death certificate was signed. In this way, a $1.1-billion corporation controlling approximately 95 percent of the North American pro wrestling market — which has seen dozens, scores, hundreds of guys and dolls pass through its revolving doors, many acquiring or worsening bad habits with virtually no institutional brakes — applies a giant coat of whitewash.

Even in the cases of genuine unknowns or minor leaguers who get glommed onto lists, legitimate concerns can be raised over "Mr." McMahon's responsibility to emit a healthier message from the top. Wrestling is about "getting over." Only a select dozen or so at any given time "get over" huge enough for past and future sacrifices to make economic sense. Yet even — no, make that *especially* — in the eye of the Benoit storm, McMahon made sure that the likes of Bobby Lashley would continue to set the standard for twenty-first-century sports entertainment. Lashley, an amateur wrestling champion at Missouri Valley College and on U.S. Army teams, is an unpolished pro ring and promo worker whose entire charisma quotient derives from a physique that not even the most gifted, driven, hardest-training jock could sustain without something extra.

In a July precursor of possible fall hearings, Democratic chairman Henry Waxman and Republican ranking minority member Tom Davis of the House Committee on Oversight and Government Reform asked WWE for, among other documents, copies of the company's studies of deaths in the industry. The congressmen will learn that there are none.

Does anyone else out there have a list? *USA Today* brushed off an old one: sixty-five wrestlers under age forty-five who died from 1987 through 1994, twenty-five of them from coronaries.

During the Benoit cable news yak-a-thon, Marc "Johnny B. Badd" Mero held up his list of the (at last count) twenty-seven deceased wrestlers he had personally had matches with.

"Except for a military person who served in Iraq, who else can say that twenty-seven work colleagues died young?" Mero asked persuasively. (Mero, who is out of the business, is saying all the right things about the problem. And since no good deed goes unpunished, defenders of the status quo do what they do, attacking his credentials and motives.)

Wrestling Observer Newsletter's Dave Meltzer, a rigorous chap, felt moved to cut through the confusion. He published a study showing sixty-two major league wrestler deaths under age fifty in the last ten years. Adjusting for the size of the talent population and the turnover, Meltzer estimated that this would be the equivalent of 435 National Football League players or 186 baseball players.

The death data in the appendix of my book *Wrestling Babylon* have been cited by another congressman, Florida Republican Cliff Stearns, who was the first to call for investigative hearings. That list, with clear criteria but admittedly incomplete, totes up, depending on interpretation, either eighty-nine or ninety-three wrestling personalities under age fifty from 1985 through 2006.

Nancy Benoit, who was retired from her career as the valet known first as Fallen Angel and later as Woman, became dead wrestling personality No. 5 since *Wrestling Babylon* went to press at the end of 2006. Chris Benoit was No. 6. Most recently, as this book headed to press, Brian "Demolition Crush" Adams (heart attack for a notorious steroid abuser) became No. 10.

Other deaths so far in 2007:

Scott "Bam Bam" Bigelow, forty-five (heart attack caused by cocaine, anti-anxiety drugs, and painkillers). Bigelow headlined against NFL legend Lawrence Taylor at *WrestleMania XI* in 1995. Is that WWE enough for you?

Michael Alfonso ("Mike Awesome"), forty-two (suicide by a former heavy steroid user). Alfonso was a star of Paul Heyman's original ECW and a cousin of Hulk Hogan.

Sherri Russell ("Sensational Sherri"), forty-nine (likely prescription pill overdose). Russell was on top as a wrestler in the women's division and later was regarded as one of the all-time great managers, female or male, during her WWF stint.

Shayne Bower ("Biff Wellington"), forty-four (heart attack for a heavy user of painkillers and steroids). Old Stampede Wrestling tag team partner of Benoit.

Nathan Randolph ("Moondog Nathan"), thirty-seven (heart attack). Veteran of independent promotions in Tennessee.

George Caiazzo ("John Kronus"), thirty-eight (likely painkiller overdose). Tag team champ in the old ECW.

Yes, every death was a unique event — and every unhappy family is unhappy in a different way and for a different reason. But you have to be blinder than The Junkyard Dog in New Orleans and more stubborn than a Missouri mule if you think the pattern is either mistakable or somehow *less* damning because of the preponderance of talent below the current pinnacle of the profession. You're also nuts if you believe that Chris Benoit was a clean liver with a clean liver or that any of these individuals died from toxic reactions to mother's milk. And if Daniel Benoit was injected with human growth hormone, it wasn't because he fell on a needle; his dad had a complex about size.

With characteristic imprecision, many in the media fingered "roid rage" for the demise of the Benoits. Wrestling weasels the world over howled in outrage. Confronting the media throng outside Nancy and Daniel's funeral in Florida, WWE announcer Jim Ross proved that he is wildly overrated when it comes to straight shooting. The compulsively folksy JR armed himself with a good ole country sound bite: "This is not a steroid issue. That horse has got to be put in the barn and unsaddled."

And indeed, for all we'll ever know, the Benoits' was a classic outbreak of domestic violence in which the pressures and chemicals of wrestling played only an incidental role. Don't count me among the weasels, though. Wrestling is a lowest-common-denominator enterprise, and the tabloid reporting, for all its flaws, contains a lowest-common-denominator truth, an undeniable rough justice. Wrestling had an appointment with

a train wreck at the Benoit level. While The Canadian Crippler may have dug particularly deep for his final spectacular high spot, the result handed his sport and lifelong obsession a long-overdue poster boy for its criminal element.

There is even speculation that Benoit wanted it that way. One of the postmortem mysteries is why he destroyed so much evidence, such as his own diaries and Nancy's old photos of the aftermath of his physical abuse of her — but not the steroids. From Bruiser Brody (who flushed David Von Erich's Placidyl supply down the toilet before the authorities arrived) to the first boys who discovered Eddie Guerrero's body, wrestlers who are "protective of the business" know that the drug traces are the first things you hide.

The culprit isn't steroids *per se*. But try "steroids-plus," a cocktail also including painkillers, muscle relaxants, sleeping pills, and all manner of over-the-counter and prescription drugs, along with cocaine, GBH, and other street drugs. Add a dollop of too much money, mal-distributed. And for good measure, stir in an essential last ingredient: groveling addiction to a peculiar life that knows no boundaries, seems to have lost all its moorings to bottom-line human values, and swears allegiance only to a decadent abstraction known as *The Business*.

Whose business?

Perhaps the only taboo still open for discussion is how to grapple with religion and its discontents.

As performers, sports entertainers are a spirited bunch. As private people, they have provided their share, or a little more, of spirituality in every variety — actual, fake, and wannabe. There is no known commandment "Thou shalt be a carny con man," but anyone hoping this would impart modesty in matters of sin and the Almighty is apt to be disappointed. Excess begets excess; many of these guys, either shamelessly or mindlessly, transfer bombastic baggage from the promo to the pulpit, only too eager to draw links between what they do or did for a buck and what they profess to believe — and most gratingly, what they demand that the rest of us believe. Pieces of the Benoit story underscore the illogic and chicanery of these *à la carte* eschatalogues.

The first wrestler-turned-evangelist I can remember was John Paul Henning, a headliner in some territories in the 1960s. Famously, the Von Erichs exploited televangelism production values and content on their strange 1980s magic carpet ride; they went so far as to emanate from a Christian Broadcasting Network affiliate before crashing and burning even more apocalyptically than fellow emotional grifters Jimmy Swaggart and Jim and Tammy Faye Bakker.

By the 1990s, Tully Blanchard was on the preacher circuit after ending his wrestling career. Kind of, sort of. Like old soldiers, wrestlers just fade away, or at least begin exercising more discretion with their indie bookings.

But the weirdness was just beginning. In those days, WWF television briefly featured Bruce Prichard's parody of a preacher, Brother Love, which was so spot-on that if you tuned in at the middle of one of his segments on a Sunday morning, without knowing his character's name or that he was spouting on a wrestling show, you would have sworn you'd landed, Borat-like, at the Universal Church of the Bewildered. During the same period, WWF also gave us Ken Johnson ("Slick"), a heel manager with the stylings of a pimp, who left to become a minister in real life and periodically returned as a wrestling character playing a minister who used to play a wrestling character. Dubious theology, cutting-edge art.

The most recent example of a smooth transition to the soul-saving dodge was by Ted DiBiase. Laid low by the excesses of the wrestling lifestyle, DiBiase — stepson of "Iron" Mike DiBiase, who died of a heart attack in the ring in 1969 — had a born-again vision and became a man of the cloth. Talent being the fungible commodity it is, the erstwhile Million Dollar Man was enlisted in the cast of thousands for the climax of the June 2007 angle in which a bomb inside Vince McMahon's limousine was said to have blown the chairman all the way from Wilkes-Barre, Pennsylvania, to the afterlife. Thus, by the will of the Lord — the lord of the rings, that is — DiBiase found himself on June 25 at the American Bank Center in Corpus Christi, Texas, for the *Raw* shoot that wound up canceled after the Benoit family's bodies were discovered.

Masters of synergy, WWE asked DiBiase to serve as a point person in grief counseling. He obliged. As fellow evangelical Bill Watts might have put it, "Worked death, shoot death . . . it's still a competition."

Nor was the Reverend Ted finished rendering unto Caesar. When WWE went into full-bore damage control two weeks later, providing a panel of authorities for talk-show shill Larry King, DiBiase was at the ready, joining the "amen" corner of wrestlers and ex-wrestlers there to assure one and all that the Benoit tragedy, impenetrably mysterious, finally just had to be chalked up to the dreaded Personal Responsibility Principle.

Unlike others on the King set, DiBiase was neither a current star on top (John Cena) nor a pathetic supplicant for a new job underneath (Chris Jericho). Later he bristled at the suggestion that he had parroted the party line so as to grease the wheels for a son in training to have his own shot at fame and riches.

In the religious sphere, as in others, Benoit himself left an ambiguous trail. After the February 2006 death of close confidante Michael "Johnny Grunge" Durham, an embittered Benoit told friends he was swearing off all confessional crutches. Later, however, as his own life went into the last throes of crisis, he was said to have found comfort again in religion, whatever that meant. He left Bibles next to the corpses of his wife and son, whatever *that* meant. We also know that Daniel had attended kindergarten at a local Baptist school, by all accounts a good one.

~

We've reached the point in the tale where your somber interlocutor is supposed to appeal to everyone's statesmanship and love of the game. This is part of the ritual of reestablishing bona fides, lest one gets labeled a nerd or a nostalgist.

Well, pardon me while I tag out. It's time for a history lesson.

Cable television, home video, and pay-per-view weren't inventions of World Wrestling Entertainment, the World Wrestling Federation, the World Wide Wrestling Federation, or the World Wildlife Fund. They were technological innovations, which created new opportunities for pro wrestling to anchor a global marketing base.

And the National Wrestling Alliance (NWA), which my uncle Sam Muchnick led through most of the previous era, wasn't exactly a haven in a heartless world. In the morphology of the wrestling economy, the NWA represented the stage of feudalism, whose closest model was the Mafia.

In 1982, Vinnie McMahon — "Junior," as Bruno Sammartino and the rest of the boys knew him, freezing their first impressions of him as a hanger-on, a green TV announcer, a product of nepotism, and ignoring what already was his impressive emergence as a showman — bought the family business. Any other promoter from the populous, media-saturated northeast territory, even one of more modest ambition and stricter ethics, would have had to face some form of the continental war that McMahon participated in, partially precipitated, and won.

Wrestling got bigger than ever. The WWF landed on the over-the-air networks, even in prime time. At different points it carried on its back two otherwise struggling TV brands, USA cable and UPN. McMahon and Martha Stewart took their companies public the same week; in the biggest upset since the arrival of the 1-2-3 Kid, Stewart would be the first of them to do jail time. McMahon made the Forbes 400 list of wealthiest Americans. He was a billionaire on paper for a while, and could become so again.

Even more extraordinary than wrestling's getting big was the sense that wrestling style — wrestling *values* — were insinuating themselves into legit sports, mainstream society, the civic conversation. Remember, kayfabe was sacrificed in large part because McMahon wanted to get out from under state athletic commission scrutiny and, especially, taxes, an effort perfectly in keeping with the antiregulatory climate in the business world in general. Wrestlers branched out into the governor's mansion and the top billing in movies, and in truth you couldn't determine which career trajectory was more substantive. Advertorial ruled; little was said or done anywhere for its intrinsic purpose, only for its angle or agenda, and the louder the better. Even democratic elections became like championship belts, a puppet-stringed distraction from a larger plot. Anthropologists of the future will decide that this was appropriate, for American society was in decay, and historian Edward Gibbon reminded us that the last spasms of empire are marked by bread and circuses.

Vince McMahon didn't invent steroids. Some East German distant cousin of Dr. Strangelove did that in the days when the Olympics were a platform of the Cold War. Athletic competition being what it is, the spread of drugs of all kinds

Benoit backdrops Goldie Rogers.

for performance enhancement, real or imagined, was inevitable and will continue to get more creepy and baroque. But here wrestling had an advantage over real sports, an advantage that would turn into a curse. For wrestling "performance" isn't about the objective feat; it's all about the subjective cosmetics, without so much as the pretense of an outside standard or a higher authority.

Even so, *sports entertainment* had image considerations, sponsors to placate, sponsors who from time to time felt the heat from forces such as the Parents Television Council. And so, over the years, WWE and its preceding entities had no choice other than to take three significant swings at drug testing, all three of which now lay exposed as swings and misses at best, perpetrated frauds at worst.

The first swing, private and unannounced, came after the Iron Sheik and "Hacksaw" Jim Duggan got busted for drug possession while driving together in New Jersey in 1987. The inside joke at the time was that the WWF's program provided for suspension if a wrestler tested positive for cocaine or negative for steroids.

The second swing was in 1991, with fanfare, after WWF steroid connection Dr. George Zahorian got trundled off to federal prison. That effort was ended within five years by a combination of lack of public interest and the need for cost cutting, as business took a downturn and McMahon faced a renewed challenge from Ted Turner's WCW. (Most of the guys caught and disciplined were example-setters in the middle of the pack. What, you thought they were going to go to the trouble of rewriting the script for the guys on top?)

The third swinging strike, the "wellness" policy, was instituted after Eddie Guerrero died, and it now looks about as authentic as that old Intercontinental Championship tournament in Rio de Janeiro. Benoit passed his WWE drug test on April 10, 2007, at a moment when Dr. Phil Astin was prescribing him a ten-month supply of steroids every three to four weeks. The July toxicology report would show that Benoit's system had about ten times the normal proportion of testosterone.

Ladies and gentlemen, no wrestling fan can ever know why Chris Benoit took his wife's life, then their child's, then his own. But wrestling fans know or should know all these other things. And unless they've sunk completely to that lowest of life forms, the markiest of marks, they have to decide consciously if the human toll of this regional carnival demimonde's transformation into an international merchandising juggernaut is any longer sustainable, acceptable, or fun.

ABOUT THE AUTHORS

Steven Johnson is co-author of *The Pro Wrestling Hall of Fame: The Tag Teams* and *The Pro Wrestling Hall of Fame: The Heels.* He holds a doctorate from the University of Virginia and has been a reporter and editor at several newspapers in Virginia, winning investigative and general news writing awards. He also contributes to SLAM! Wrestling, *restling Revue*, and other publications.

Heath McCoy has been hooked on pro wrestling since he first discovered Stampede Wrestling at the age of ten while flipping through the channels one Saturday afternoon in his Saskatoon home. Author of the acclaimed *Pain and Passion: The History of Stampede Wrestling*, McCoy is also an award-winning pop culture columnist and reporter for the *Calgary Herald*, a beat that has led him to extensively cover Stampede Wrestling — the Western Canadian promotion run by the legendary Hart family — where Chris Benoit broke into the business in the mid-1980s.

Irvin Muchnick is the author of *Wrestling Babylon: Piledriving Tales of Drugs, Sex, Death, and Scandal* and the forthcoming *Chris and Nancy: The True Story of the Benoit Murder-Suicide and Pro Wrestling's Cocktail of Death*, both from ECW Press.

Greg Oliver is a writer and editor from Toronto. He is the author of *The Pro Wrestling Hall of Fame: The Canadians,* and co-author of both *The Pro Wrestling Hall of Fame: The Tag Teams* and *The Pro Wrestling Hall of Fame: The Heels.* Oliver has covered pro wrestling for more than 20 years through the SLAM! Wrestling Web site, the *Canadian Wrestling Report* newsletter, magazines and newspapers.